HISTORY & GEOGRAPHY 1006
The Age of Revolution

LIFEPAC Test is located in the center of the booklet. Please remove before starting the unit.

Author:
William A. Alexander

Editor-in-Chief:
Richard W. Wheeler, M.A.Ed.

Editors:
J. Douglas Williamson
Richard R. Anderson, M.A.

Consulting Editor:
Howard Stitt, Th.M Ed.D.

Revision Editor:
Alan Christopherson, M.S.

MEDIA CREDITS:
Page 7: © NCarter-Img, iStock, Thinkstock; **10:** © Tony Baggett, iStock, Thinkstock; **13:** © John Michael Wright; © John De Critz the Elder; © Sir Godfrey Kneller; © William Wissing © Sir Anthony Van Dyck; **27:** © Photos.com, Thinkstock; **29:** © flySnow, iStock, Thinkstock; **30:** © Charles Édouard Armand-Dumaresq, White House Cabinet Room; **31:** © Steven Wynn, iStock, Thinkstock; **32,47:** © Photos.com, Thinkstock; **46,52:** © GeorgiosArt, iStock, Thinkstock; **51:** © Micha Rosenwirth, iStock, Thinkstock; **57:** © Rubens Alarcon, Hemera, Thinkstock; **58:** © Rene Drouyer, Hermera, Thinkstock.

804 N. 2nd Ave. E.
Rock Rapids, IA 51246-1759

The Age of Revolution

Introduction

The concept of man's natural right to self-government began at a time of sovereign rule and monarchical dominance. This concept spread rapidly from country to country, contributing to revolts against autocratic governments, first in England, then in America, and later in France.

In this LIFEPAC® you will study the age of revolution as it unfolded in these three nations. Examining each country's background, you will observe the growing turbulence that contributed to the people's revolt. You will learn of the struggles and conflicts of the people in their fervor for self-rule, noting their gradual victories in obtaining their God-given rights. Finally, you will study the effects each revolution had in the daily lives of the citizens of the country involved and in the lives of people around the world.

Historians are concerned with understanding the events which shaped our world. The national revolutions you are about to study did much to make our world what it is today. By studying this unit you will better appreciate the sacrifices and hardships of our Founding Fathers and of those of England and France who persevered for the freedoms we often take for granted today.

Objectives

Read these objectives. The objectives tell you what you will be able to do when you have successfully completed this LIFEPAC. When you have finished this LIFEPAC, you should be able to:

1. Outline the factors leading to the English Revolution.

2. Describe the Roundhead victory under Cromwell and the changes he brought to English government.

3. Explain the growth and philosophy of Britain's early political parties, the Whigs and the Tories.

4. Describe the growing strength of Parliament from the time of Charles II through the reign of George II.

5. Explain how England's government is now run and how her laws are passed and enforced.

6. Explain how English colonies in America were established and governed.

7. Explain how the French and Indian War gave America valuable training for war.

8. List the factors leading to the colonies' rebellion against England.

9. Describe the opposing sentiments of Americans concerning war with their mother country.

10. List the advantages and disadvantages of each side in the American Revolution.

11. Give an overview of the battles and strategies of the American Revolution from Lexington to Yorktown.

12. Describe and contrast the new governments that were established by young America.

13. Describe the factors during the reigns of Louis XV and Louis XVI which led to the people's unrest against the Old Regime and the onset of the French Revolution.

14. Describe the measures taken by the National Assembly and the reasons for its fall.

15. Explain the steps taken by the National Convention and the government of its Directory.

16. Describe the steps leading to the takeover of France by Napoleon and government under his Consulate.

17. Describe Napoleon's positive actions of reform in France.

18. Describe Napoleon's offensive for control of Europe and the steps leading to his downfall and final defeat.

Survey the LIFEPAC. Ask yourself some questions about this study and write your questions here.

_____

_____

_____

_____

_____

_____

_____

_____

_____

_____

_____

_____

_____

_____

_____

_____

_____

_____

_____

1. ENGLISH REVOLUTION

Preceding America and France by over one hundred years, England led in the age of revolutions. Revolutions are not born overnight. The events and causes which lead people to revolt often span years and even decades. Such was the case in the English Revolution.

The seventeenth century was an age of absolutism in most of the countries of Europe. However, the English kings never became as powerful as the other European **monarchs** because of the prominence of **Parliament**. Even the **Tudors**, who had almost unlimited power, had to deal with Parliament. Without the consent of Parliament, a ruler could neither make nor repeal any laws or impose new taxes. Parliament's control of the finances was an effective tool for curbing an overly ambitious king.

The Tudors shrewdly avoided conflicts with Parliament, particularly over finances. Although the Tudors acted on the principle of the **divine right** of kings, they did not emphasize it. With strong support from the middle class, the Tudors acted as they wished, and England enjoyed a long period of prosperity under their rule.

In this section you will examine the factors that lead to the English Revolution which followed the Tudor era. You will read about the **Roundhead** victory led by Oliver Cromwell and the changes he made in English government. You will examine the growth and philosophy of Britain's early political parties, the **Whigs** and the **Tories**. After studying the growing strength of Parliament from the time of Charles II through the reign of George II, you will learn how England's government is run today.

Section Objectives

Review these objectives. When you have completed this section, you should be able to:

1. Outline the factors leading to the English Revolution.

2. Describe the Roundhead victory under Cromwell and the changes he brought to English government.

3. Explain the growth and philosophy of Britain's early political parties, the Whigs and the Tories.

4. Describe the growing strength of Parliament from the time of Charles II through the reign of George II.

5. Explain how England's government is now run and how her laws are passed and enforced.

Vocabulary

Study these words to enhance your learning success in this section.

Anglican	Calvinist	Cavaliers
commonwealth	divine right	executive
monarchy	Parliament	presbyters
Roundheads	Stuart	Tories
Tudor	Whigs	

Note: *All vocabulary words in this LIFEPAC appear in* **boldface** *print the first time they are used. If you are not sure of the meaning when you are reading, study the definitions given.*

DIVINE RIGHT

England had been ruled by several monarchs who believed they had a **divine right** to absolute power and total control of the government. However, when Charles I came to the throne, that idea was challenged by the people. The followers of Charles were known as the **Cavaliers** and were opposed by the **Roundheads** led by Oliver Cromwell. The Roundheads won the rebellion. Cromwell gained control of the government and established a **commonwealth**.

Cavaliers. England in the 1500s was ruled by the **Tudor monarchy**. Although a **Parliament** existed at that time, its function was basically limited to carrying out the desires of the Tudor king or queen in power.

The last monarch of the Tudor era was Queen Elizabeth. She ruled for almost fifty years as a popular and powerful monarch. Queen Elizabeth headed a glorious era of British history.

A proud, highly intelligent woman, Elizabeth was sometimes overpowering. Although she never married, Elizabeth used her friendships with foreign ministers and ambassadors to gain political and international favors. Because of her influence, she was often able to avoid war.

England's Elizabethan period was the final chapter in the Renaissance era. During Elizabeth's reign, England produced impressive music, art, literature, and what became known as Elizabethan architecture, in spite of the disorders of the times. Certainly two of the more famous Englishmen of that time were William Shakespeare and Francis Bacon. Shakespeare's popularity was based upon his exacting and dramatic plays. His writings are still studied in many schools around the world. Bacon was a lawyer-philosopher whose well respected views were aimed at solving human problems.

Britain also became a naval power under Elizabeth. In 1588, the English navy successfully defeated the Spanish Armada, the fleet of the most powerful nation in Europe.

England's power on the ocean continued to grow throughout the Elizabethan Era and into the reign of the **Stuarts**. As the golden Elizabethan years came to a close, the troubled times that emerged made Elizabeth's reign look even more glorious and impressive.

James VI of Scotland (Elizabeth's cousin) began the Stuart line of English rulers by becoming King James I of England in 1603. His rule was plagued with difficulties from the beginning. The English citizenry looked upon James as a foreigner who really could not relate or empathize with their problems. A staunch believer in the divine right of kings, James believed that it was God's will for him to be king over England. Therefore, he expected absolute obedience to his dictates. James ruled in a prideful, cold, and tactless manner, alienating many of his subjects.

James I did not have a good relationship with Parliament. Whereas members of the House of Lords and House of Commons rarely opposed Elizabeth I, they began to offer the newcomer stiff opposition. The people and their representatives knew Elizabeth's shortcoming. However, she was popular because they also were aware of her love for them and their country. James, on the other hand, demanded that his proposals be accepted without any explanation to the Parliament or reasons to the people. James insisted that he be obeyed without offering any proof of his good will or good faith. Obviously, as Parliament refused to cooperate with him, James became furious.

As the king's troubles with Parliament grew, so did England's economic woes. Although some Englishmen were financially successful, many were encountering difficult times. Because of a dramatic shift from farming to sheep raising, many people were out of work; fewer people were needed for sheep raising than for farming. Inflation was also increasing rapidly in Great Britain by the early 1600s, casting dark shadows on England's economic scene.

During the twenty years of James' reign, he fought with the people of England and the Parliament over money, religion, and foreign affairs. Since Parliament would not grant him the money he requested, James obtained funds by selling titles of nobility and by pressuring Englishmen to make loans to him. The king made himself even more unpopular when he refused to help the German Protestants against the Catholics during the Thirty Years' War. Catholicism was immensely unpopular in England at that time and most Englishmen were Protestants. There was a large, influential group called the Puritans who were especially disturbed by this apparent friendliness toward Catholics. The Puritans wanted to purge the **Anglican** Church (the English state church) of all traces of Catholic ritual which Elizabeth had kept as a religious compromise when the country became Protestant.

James' reign, however, was not without positive accomplishments. He commissioned a new translation of the Bible. The project was vigorously supported by Puritans who provided some of the Biblical scholars who did the work. Although officially called the Authorized Version, the translation is known to most of us today as the King James Version. This translation placed God's Word in the popular language of that time and enabled many people to easily "search the scriptures."

| A Cavalier

James was followed to the English throne by his son, Charles I, in 1625. Though not the strong, personal, and popular leader the Tudors had been, Charles was a definite improvement over his father as a monarch. Yet, he too lacked insight into gaining the support of the English people. Charles became entangled with unpopular wars involving Spain and France. In raising financial support for the military, he forced wealthy citizens to loan him money. Charles also required the English people to house soldiers at the householder's expense. Finally, when Parliament offered stiff resistance to his unnecessary taxation and church policy in 1629, Charles simply dissolved Parliament.

For the next eleven years, England was ruled without a Parliament. Charles, free of the Parliament's suppressive arguments, taxed towns, levied fines, and held secret trials without a jury.

The situation deteriorated when Charles attempted to establish the **Anglican** Church in **Calvinistic** Scotland. In retaliation, a Scottish army invaded England. Desperate for finances to meet this threat, the cornered Charles had no choice but to call Parliament. Beginning in 1640, it lasted for twenty years and became known as the *Long Parliament*.

Parliament refused to give any funds to Charles unless he agreed to having limits set on his power. Charles went along for a time, but then decided he had had enough. He tried to arrest the leaders of Parliament, who were warned and thus fled. The king and parliament began to assemble men and supplies to fight. Civil war broke out between the two sides in 1642.

Supporters of the king were called Cavaliers. They consisted of Anglicans, Catholics, nobles, and other groups that tended to favor traditional power. Wearing their hair long and curled, the Cavaliers stood in contrast to their opponents, the Roundheads, who cut their hair short. The Roundheads were primarily Protestants who wanted a limited monarchy and a less Catholic Anglican church. The Puritans were the best organized and most militant of the Roundheads. They took the lead in the opposition to the king.

Complete the following sentences.

1.1   Queen Elizabeth was the last monarch of the _____ rule.

1.2   James I was the first of the _____ kings in England.

1.3   A famous writer of the Elizabethan era was _____ .

1.4   Bacon's philosophy was centered around solving _____ .

1.5   England's naval power was first established by the defeat of the _____
_____ .

1.6   A king's belief that God has willed for him to rule is known as _____ .

1.7   The Authorized Version of the Bible is commonly called the _____
_____ .

1.8   The twenty-year Parliament Charles I recalled was known as the _____
_____ .

1.9   Supporters of the king were called a. _____ ; their opponents were known
as b. _____ .

Answer true or false.

1.10   _____   The existence of Parliament under the Tudor monarchs was limited and only
necessary when the monarch desired.

1.11   _____   Parliament had unlimited power during the reign of James I and Charles I.

1.12   _____   Charles I dissolved Parliament because of strong resistance to his policies.

1.13   _____   When Ireland threatened war against Charles I, he had to recall Parliament.

1.14   _____   Civil war in England developed when Charles attempted to arrest members
of Parliament who opposed him.

Roundheads. Queen Elizabeth's father, Henry VIII, had thrown the Roman Catholic Church out of England and established the Anglican Church, the Church of England. The major difference between the Anglican Church and Catholic Church was the leadership. The sovereign of England led the Anglican Church, and the pope in Rome was the supreme leader of the Catholic Church. Elizabeth had tried to settle the issue of religion by making the Anglican Church acceptable to most of the people. It was basically Protestant in theology, but Catholic in ritual. Many people were discontent with this compromise. However, Elizabeth was tolerant of the various religious groups and kept the disagreements under control. After Elizabeth's death, the religious situation in England became increasingly unstable.

A movement arose within the Anglican Church to purify it of its Roman Catholic relics and traditions. This Puritan movement grew during the Tudor leadership of Henry and Elizabeth. By the reign of the Stuart kings, James I and Charles I, the Puritans had a very strong following in Great Britain.

The Puritans were followers of the French theologian, John Calvin. Calvinists often followed an extremely disciplined life style. Such activities as dancing, playing cards, participating in certain games, and attending the theater were considered sinful because of their worldly involvement. Calvinists in England were intent on purifying the Anglican Church. They opposed such rituals as making the sign of the cross, kneeling at communion, and the wearing of robes by the clergy.

The Puritan movement was divided into three (3) main groups largely due to preferences in church structure. The (1) *Presbyterians* wanted a state-supported church without bishops. A district and national organization was allowed, but each local congregation would elect its own **presbyters**, or elders. The (2) *Puritans* wanted to remain in the Church of England, but they wanted either to eliminate or to purify the ceremonies, doctrines, and rituals carried over from Roman Catholicism.

The third group of Calvinists was known as the (3) *Separatists*, *Independents*, or *Congregationalists*. They believed that each congregation should have the right to choose its own minister and to make its own rules. The Separatists wanted to remain separate, or independent, from any other congregation. The Pilgrims who came to America were from the Separatist group.

Calvinists in Great Britain were usually part of the growing middle class. Many Calvinists were members of the House of Commons, where they used their influence to make reforms in the Church of England. These Calvinist Puritans were the main driving force behind the Roundheads. Their leader was a stern, military-minded man named Oliver Cromwell.

Cromwell thoroughly trained his Puritan troops before leading them into combat. His troops, the "ironsides," went into battle against the more flamboyant, but poorly trained Cavaliers. The Puritans were confident that God ordained them to conquer the Cavaliers. The Roundheads often sang hymns and Psalms as they entered battle. The following hymn was probably one of those sung by the Calvinists as their battle cry.

| The Austere Puritan

A Mighty Fortress Is Our God

A mighty fortress is our God,
A bulwark never failing;
Our helper He, amid the flood
Of mortal ills prevailing.
For still our ancient foe
Doth seek to work us woe;
His craft and power are great,
And, armed with cruel hate,
On earth is not his equal.

And though this world,
With devils filled,
Should threaten to undo us,
We will not fear,
For God hath willed
His truth to triumph thru us.
The prince of darkness grim
We tremble not for him;
His rage we can endure,
For lo! his doom is sure,
One little word shall fell him.

The Cavaliers were no match for Cromwell's well disciplined, motivated troops. Following defeats in two major battles, Charles I surrendered. Cromwell, backed by his army of independent Calvinists, assumed control of the new government. The army drove all of the Anglicans and Presbyterians out of Parliament. This action became known as *Pride's Purge* because the soldiers enforcing the action were led by Colonel Pride. It left the parliament firmly in the control of Cromwell's supporters.

The House of Lords and the monarchy were abolished by the new "Rump Parliament." England was proclaimed a commonwealth. Charles I was tried by a special court and beheaded in 1649. His family fled to Europe to live. In place of Charles, Oliver Cromwell became the military dictator of England. In 1653, Cromwell dismissed Parliament, abolished the commonwealth, and was named Lord Protector of the country.

Cromwell was a separatist Puritan who had a reputation of being trustworthy. His keen military mind was also used quite well in politics. The bold Calvinist was an excellent public speaker and an able statesman. Cromwell wanted his government to help the English people by improving manufacturing and trade.

When rebellions arose in Scotland and Ireland, Cromwell moved quickly and harshly to stop them. The people of both Scotland and Ireland came to hate him. Cromwell was respected, but he never became a very popular ruler in England because of his harsh methods and hard ways.

Cromwell died in 1658 without choosing or training an able successor. His son, Richard, assumed the role of Lord Protector. However, he was not as capable as his father and was over-thrown by the military. Finally in 1660, a new Parliament invited Charles I's son, Charles II, to return to England as king.

Identify the following names.

1.15 Calvinists _____

_____

1.16 Puritans _____

_____

1.17 Presbyterians _____

_____

1.18 Separatists _____

_____

1.19 Pride's Purge _____

_____

1.20 ironsides _____

_____

1.21 Cromwell _____

_____

Complete the following activities.

1.22 Describe the religious climate of England under the following rulers.

a. Henry VIII _____

_____

b. Elizabeth I _____

_____

c. James I and Charles I _____

_____

1.23 State the reasons for the Roundhead victory over the Cavaliers.

_____

_____

_____

_____

Answer the following questions.

1.24 What three major changes in England's government did Cromwell make?

a. _____

_____

b. _____

_____

c. _____

_____

1.25 Which of Cromwell's traits worked

a. to his advantage as ruler? _____

_____

b. to his disadvantage as ruler? _____

_____

PEOPLE'S CHOICE

Monarchy returns. As the eldest of Charles I's two sons, Charles II restored the Stuart line to the throne. Charles was well aware of the fact that he had to be careful in dealing with Parliament. When Parliament opposed his ideas, Charles tried to gain his objectives by other methods. The result was a division of power between the king and the parliament.

Charles II had Catholic leanings all of his life and became a Catholic on his deathbed. English Catholics had been some of his most faithful supporters during the dark years of his exile. They had helped him to escape Cromwell's army after the last defeat of the Cavaliers. Moreover, the king's brother, James, was openly Catholic.

Charles kept his opinions secret because of the intense English resentment toward Rome. What little legislation he tried to pass in support of Catholicism was met with defeat.

Parliament had learned some bitter lessons. They had become firmly anti-Catholic and anti-Calvinist. The Anglican Church was once again strong and controlled organized religion in England. Knowing that Charles II's brother, James, would become the next king, the House of Commons passed a bill that would have prevented a Roman Catholic from becoming king of England. Although the House of Lords rejected the bill, the people's opinion on the issue had been made quite clear.

James I

Charles I

Charles II

James II

William III

Mary II

| English Monarchs

Under King Charles II, Parliament was divided into two groups of almost equal strength. On the one side were the **Tories**, strong supporters of the Anglican Church, who wanted a strong hereditary king without absolute power. The opposing side, the **Whigs**, wanted a king who was merely a figurehead, allowing the real power to be held by Parliament, thus giving more power to Protestants not belonging to the Church of England. These two groups marked the establishment of organized political parties in Great Britain.

One very important piece of legislation was passed under Charles II. The Habeas Corpus Act, which was passed by Parliament in 1679, was a major accomplishment in the area of law and human rights. This act stated that any person arrested and imprisoned must be brought before a judge within twenty days. This eliminated secret arrests and trials for enemies of the king and government.

James II came to the throne following the death of his brother in 1685. James had little regard for what Parliament thought. Unlike Charles, James was quite bold in his Catholicism and insisted on being king by divine right. His obnoxious attitude made him many enemies in both the Whig Party and the Tory Party.

James' second wife gave birth to a son in 1688. This meant that there would be a Catholic heir to the throne. That threat united the Parliament against the monarch. To eliminate the possibility of a continued reign by the Catholic Stuarts, Parliament invited William III of Holland and his wife, Mary (the Protestant daughter of James by his first wife) to rule together over England. William came to England and James fled to France. Great Britain once again was ruled by Protestant monarchs. This revolution was known as the Glorious Revolution because not one shot was fired.

Before taking office, William and Mary were required to sign a very important and significant document in British and American history, the 1689 Bill of Rights. It stated that the king was merely an official chosen by Parliament and subject to its laws. The bill also protected the rights of individual citizens. Such privileges as freedom of speech, opportunity of a fair trial, and protection against cruel treatment by public officials were guaranteed. The bill greatly increased the power of Parliament and also went far in securing the personal rights of the people.

The Act of Toleration was also passed by Parliament in 1689. This act protected non-Anglican Protestants and allowed them to worship freely, thus ending the years of persecution and prejudice. A later act passed by Parliament, the Act of Settlement, contained a provision whereby Mary's sister Anne would succeed William and Mary to the throne should the two rulers not have heirs of their own. If Anne were unable to assume the English rulership, then Sophia of Hanover, a German princess who was the Protestant granddaughter of James I, would become queen. Parliament took these steps to block the Catholic Stuart relatives of James II from ever again occupying the English throne.

Thus, England changed, by civil war and political maneuvering, from an absolute monarchy to a constitutional monarchy. The people gained control of the king and began to assert their own rights as individuals.

Complete the following activities.

1.26 Give the political beliefs of the two groups of Parliament under Charles II.

a. Whigs _____

_____

b. Tories _____

_____

1.27 How did Charles II and James II differ in the way they approached Parliament?

_____

_____

_____

_____

1.28 William and Mary were brought to English rule.

Why? _____

How? _____

What gave them the right? _____

Match the following items.

1.29 _____ fair trials

1.30 _____ free speech

1.31 _____ no Catholic Stuart king or queen

1.32 _____ arrested person brought to trial within twenty days

1.33 _____ non-Anglican Protestants given freedom of religion

1.34 _____ protection from cruel treatment

1.35 _____ privileges of English citizens

a. Habeas Corpus Act

b. Bill of Rights

c. Act of Toleration

d. Act of Settlement

Complete the following activity.

1.36 If you had lived under the rule of Charles II, would you have been a Whig or a Tory? Back your answer with reasons supporting your position. Compare your answer with that of a classmate.

_____

_____

_____

_____

_____

_____

_____

_____

_____

_____

_____

_____

TEACHER CHECK _____ _____

initials   date

Parliament rules. The signing of the Bill of Rights in 1689 marked the end of the English Revolution which had begun in 1603. The struggle between the throne and Parliament was to determine who would rule England—the king or Parliament. Parliament was the victor.

This victory, however, did not ensure a democracy for Great Britain. Parliament was not a true representative of all the people. The House of Lords consisted of the clergy and selected nobles. The House of Commons, politically more powerful than the House of Lords, was largely composed of middle-class citizens. The working class received little representation.

William III, being from Holland, knew little of England's domestic problems. His chief interest was in competing with Louis XIV of France in European affairs. However, William made some very wise decisions. He selected competent advisors to aid him in making decisions on how to run the country. He allowed Parliament to rule almost unopposed in domestic situations in return for a freer hand in conducting foreign problems. Williams' ministers also joined the House of Commons, thus adding to his support within that lawmaking body.

Parliament continued to gain power under William's reign. Parliament was given the right to declare war and to remove unworthy judges, an action previously taken only by the monarch. The power of the throne to veto acts of Parliament gradually faded out of existence, giving Parliament an even freer rein. After the death of Mary II in 1694, William III ruled alone until his death in 1702 and was succeeded by Queen Anne (1702-14), the Protestant sister of Mary II and the last of the Stuart rulers.

Queen Anne died childless; and George I, the son of Sophia of Hanover, took the throne. He was followed by his son George II. Since both were German born, they cared little about Great Britain's domestic situation. Their disinterest only strengthened the growing power of Parliament's rule.

One outstanding member of the Whig Party elected to Parliament was Sir Robert Walpole. He became the leader of the Whig Party in the House of Commons. Because of the king's lack of interest in ruling English affairs, Walpole was recognized as first, or prime, minister responsible for the functions of the government. This initiated a political position which has carried through to this century. The prime minister is the true head of English government today; however, he brings the ruler's ideas to the cabinet and Parliament.

When a prime minister is no longer part of the majority party in the House of Commons, he is replaced by the king's selection of a new prime minister. This choice is always the recognized leader of the majority party. The cabinet, part of the **executive** branch of government, advises the prime minister on domestic and foreign affairs, and is selected by the prime minister.

England has preserved its tradition of royalty. The formality of serving in the name of his or her majesty still prevails in Great Britain. The king or queen continues to open each session of Parliament with a speech that introduces the proposed legislative agenda. However, this address is a formality, for the cabinet writes the speech and lists the laws it feels are necessary. Parliament is the body that passes the laws; and the cabinet, under the prime minister, upholds and enforces them.

The Parliamentary system revolutionized government in Great Britain. It was vastly different from the absolute monarchy of the Tudor Era. Bestowing new rights and freedoms to her citizenry, the English Revolution placed the reins of British power in the hands of Parliament and gave her people a welcome voice in determining their future.

Write the letters for the correct answer on each line (more than one letter will be required for each answer).

1.37 Representatives in Parliament included _____ .

a. clergy   b. working class   c. middle class   d. nobles

1.38 Branches of Parliament include _____ .

a. prime minister   b. House of Lords
c. House of Representatives   d. House of Commons

1.39 Wise decisions by William III included _____ .

a. selecting wise advisors
b. giving Parliament rule at home
c. having his ministers join the House of Commons
d. letting Parliament handle foreign affairs

1.40 British rulers who cared little about English domestic affairs were _____ .

a. George I   b. William III   c. George II   d. Charles II

1.41 Increased power for Parliament included the _____ .

a. right to declare war   b. fading of king's veto power
c. right to chose a monarch   d. right to remove unworthy judges

Answer the following questions.

1.42 Why was Parliament not a true representation of the people? _____

_____

1.43 How are English laws

a. introduced? _____

b. passed? _____

c. enforced? _____

1.44 Write the answers to these questions concerning England's prime minister.

a. What are his duties? _____

b. When is he replaced? _____

c. How is he replaced? _____

d. Who is chosen in his place? _____

Review the material in this section in preparation for the Self Test. The Self Test will check your mastery of this particular section. The items missed on this Self Test will indicate specific areas where restudy is needed for mastery.

SELF TEST 1

Match the following items (each answer, 2 points).

1.01	_____	Cavaliers
1.02	_____	Whigs
1.03	_____	Calvinist
1.04	_____	Roundheads
1.05	_____	Tories
1.06	_____	ironsides
1.07	_____	Parliament
1.08	_____	divine right
1.09	_____	Stuart
1.010	_____	Tudor

a. nickname for Cromwell's troops

b. Puritans' and Presbyterians' religious belief

c. supporters of Charles I in the civil war

d. Queen Elizabeth's royal line

e. House of Representatives

f. opponents of Charles I, led by Cromwell

g. party wanting strong English king under Charles II

h. God's will to rule

i. party wanting powerful Parliament under Charles II

j. legislative body of England

k. line of kings begun by James I

Complete the following sentences (each answer, 3 points).

1.011 Government by a hereditary ruler is called a(n) _____ .

1.012 The leader of the Roundhead victory over the Cavaliers was _____
_____ .

1.013 Britain became a naval power after the defeat of the _____
_____ .

1.014 Three Calvinist groups were the Puritans, the a. _____ ,
and the b. _____ .

1.015 Cromwell ruled over England as a(n) _____ .

1.016 England's political parties came from the a. _____ and b. _____ .

1.017 James II caused problems during his reign because of his _____ religion.

1.018 The Protestant rulers who replaced James II were _____ .

1.019 The English Revolution put _____ in control of British affairs.

1.020 The two houses of Parliament are a. _____ and

b. _____ .

Answer true or false (each answer, 1 point).

1.021 _____ Parliament rarely opposed Queen Elizabeth's rulings.

1.022 _____ Charles I dissolved Parliament because of war with Scotland.

1.023 _____ James I sparked the English Revolution by attempting to arrest his House of Commons enemies.

1.024 _____ The Church of England was established under Henry VIII.

1.025 _____ Cromwell left no able leader to take his place.

1.026 _____ The Habeas Corpus Act assured trial within twenty days.

1.027 _____ The Act of Settlement secured important personal rights for English citizens.

1.028 _____ Parliament gained power with the fading of the king's veto power.

1.029 _____ Sir Robert Walpole was the first British prime minister.

1.030 _____ Today, Britain's monarch is mainly a figurehead of tradition.

Write the letter for the correct answer on each line (each answer, 2 points).

1.031 When Charles I sent troops into the House of Commons, this action resulted in open

warfare in the _____ .
a. War of Roses
b. English Revolution
c. English Bill of Rights
d. American Revolution

1.032 James I encountered problems with _____ .
a. Scotland
b. Parliament
c. the prime minister
d. France

1.033 Oliver Cromwell made changes in the government by abolishing _____ .
a. the office of prime minister
b. the House of Commons
c. the House of Lords
d. both houses of Parliament

1.034 The British prime minister brings the kings' desires to _____ .
a. the House of Lords
b. the House of Commons
c. the people
d. the Parliament

1.035 At the end of the English Revolution, changes included the _____ .
a. Bill of Rights
b. Magna Carta
c. Declaration of Independence
d. Petition of Right

1.036 Parliament had very limited power under the _____ .

    a. Tudors   b. Stuarts   c. Hapsburgs   d. Tories

Complete the following activities (each answer, 4 points).

1.037 Describe the political parties of England and their basic political stands under Charles II.

    a. _____

    _____

    _____

    b. _____

    _____

    _____

1.038 Describe the membership of the following branches of English government and give their duties.

    a. House of Lords _____

    _____

    b. House of Commons _____

    _____

    c. prime minister _____

    _____

81 / 101   SCORE _____   TEACHER _____ _____

                                                      initials   date

2. AMERICAN REVOLUTION

The road to revolution in America began with the establishment of the first English colony at Jamestown in 1607. During the sixteenth and seventeenth centuries the English had to contend with the Spanish and Dutch for colonies in North America. However, in the eighteenth century the greatest threat to the English colonies came from the French. The French were finally defeated in a series of wars, the last of which was the French and Indian War (1754-1763). The wars established Britain as the dominant power in America, but they were also very expensive. The thirteen English colonies were now asked to pay for the war that had been fought to protect them from the French. This was the spark that started the American revolt.

The French and Indian War also helped to prepare the American colonists. They received some valuable training during the war. They learned to fight in the manner of the Native Americans, and they learned battlefield tactics. Some of the young men also received valuable training as officers. These experiences were to prove priceless in the Revolution.

The American Revolution began on May 15, 1775 at Lexington and ended with the final English surrender at Yorktown in 1781. The foundation of the United States was laid in two important documents: the Declaration of Independence and the Constitution. The Declaration of Independence was signed in 1776, giving the legal framework for the Revolution. The Constitution was enacted in 1789, giving a strong structure to the country's hard-won freedom.

Section Objectives

Review these objectives. When you have completed this section, you should be able to:

6. Explain how English colonies in America were established and governed.

7. Explain how the French and Indian War gave America valuable training for war.

8. List the factors leading to the colonies' rebellion against England.

9. Describe the opposing sentiments of Americans concerning war with their mother country.

10. List the advantages and disadvantages of each side in the American Revolution.

11. Give an overview of the battles and strategies of the American Revolution from Lexington to Yorktown.

12. Describe and contrast the new governments that were established by young America.

Vocabulary

Study these words to enhance your learning success in this section.

judicial	legislative	mercantilism
militia	proprietor	

BRITISH BACKGROUND

Beginning with the founding of Jamestown in 1607, England established thirteen colonies along the Atlantic coast from Maine to Florida. The French in Canada and in the Ohio valley, and the Spanish in Florida, considered the English colonies a threat to their territorial interests in North America. The movement of English settlers into the Ohio valley brought conflict with the French.

In 1754 the French and Indian War, part of a larger French-British struggle for empires, began in the colonies. Some of the American colonists fought with the British to protect their homes. By 1763 England had defeated France and her allies. By the terms of the Treaty of Paris, Britain took Canada and the Ohio valley from the French and Florida from the Spanish. However, the victory caused a division between England and her American colonies. The British crown attempted to extract the cost of the war from the colonies through various taxes. This led to open dissension in the colonies and eventually to revolution.

Establishment of colonies. English colonization of the New World began when Virginia was established as a British colony in 1607. Dotting the Atlantic coastline from Maine to Georgia, thirteen colonies had been established by 1750. Many of these colonies were founded by private English citizens who formed companies to reap financial profits from the development of New World territories. Some wealthy Englishmen bought huge tracts of land from the king, while others were given land in payment of debts or in exchange for various favors performed for the crown. Royal charters were issued by the king, giving stockholders, companies, or **proprietors** the authority to govern and carry out their adventures for anticipated monetary gains. Charters also guaranteed that every colonist in America would be considered an Englishman, entitled to the same legal rights and privileges enjoyed by British citizens in the homeland. These charters were exceptionally valuable to the colonists as a legal basis for their struggle with the mother country.

Actually, the colonies were never as profitable to investors as was initially hoped. However, interest in traveling to the New World was encouraged in England, especially among the middle and lower classes. The continuous political upheaval between the Stuarts and Parliament; religious friction among the Anglicans, Puritans, and Catholics; and poor economic conditions gave thousands of people good reason to look for something better in the American wilderness.

The decision to move to the New World was not an easy one. Life for most newcomers was difficult, trying, and far more dangerous than in England. Thick forests covered the countryside, creating the awesome task of clearing land for homes, farms, and gardens. Because of the climate, time was short for growing the desperately needed food for enduring the hard first winter ahead. The Native Americans were not always welcoming to the British. Some did help early settlers, but most Native Americans resented the threatening foreigners who were taking their camping and hunting grounds.

From the beginning, the people of the colonies were allowed a voice in their government. By the middle of the eighteenth century, each colony had a governor, an advisory council to the governor, and an assembly that served as a voice for the people. The structure was similar to England's and served its purpose well in the early years of the colonies. Gradually, however, England tried to exercise greater control over the colonies, especially in regulating and interfering with America's growing economy.

Much of this interference began under the rule of Oliver Cromwell, who attempted to prevent Dutch ships from trading with the colonies. Cromwell also tried to enforce the principle of

mercantilism, insisting that a colony should help support the mother country by giving her an abundant percentage of its raw materials and by buying a large share of the manufactured goods produced in the mother country. At the same time, the mother country discouraged buying and selling with other countries without special approval.

English trade acts, based upon the theory of mercantilism, stated that products shipped from the colonies had to be transported by English ships with English crews. Also, a large amount of colonial products could only be sold in Great Britain, discouraging many businessmen from putting forth their best effort in manufacturing goods. The English trade acts further stated that goods sold to the colonies from other European countries first had to be inspected and taxed in England before being shipped to the colonies.

These trade laws were enforced by English officials, called revenue agents, who were appointed by the king's governors. Violators were brought to trial before judges, also appointed by the king, who decided the cases without juries. Writs of Assistance allowed English officials to search anywhere at anytime without any safeguards against abuse. It was the trial without juries that seriously rankled the colonists. Trial by jury was a traditional right of Englishmen guaranteed by British law and custom. That meant it was also guaranteed by their colonial charters.

The English government claimed these actions were necessary to stop smuggling and other offenses. The colonists insisted that their guaranteed rights as Englishmen were being abused. Citizens in England had the right of trial by jury and the protection of their private property against searches without written warrants. The American colonists believed they, as English subjects living abroad, should have these same rights.

The trade laws were immensely unpopular in America. They were regularly avoided and only sporadically enforced before the French and Indian War. Smuggling goods directly to the colonies on foreign ships was common and accepted. The laws failed to generate any substantial income for the mother country, but they did generate a great deal of ill will and conflict.

Write the correct answer in each blank.

2.1 English colonization in the New World began with the establishment of

a. _____ in the year b. _____ .

2.2 The documents that allowed the English to search anywhere at anytime were known as the

_____ .

2.3 English _____ stifled the colonies' ability to trade in their own way.

2.4 Colonists had been guaranteed the same rights as a. _____

in the king's b. _____ .

Write the letter for the correct answer on each line.

2.5 American colonies were founded by _____ .
a. companies, the Parliament, and wealthy Englishmen
b. companies, the king, and freed slaves
c. the king, proprietors, and Parliament
d. companies, proprietors, and wealthy Englishmen

2.6 Wealthy Englishmen received land in America _____ .
a. by purchasing it from the king, in payment of a debt, or in return for a favor to the king
b. by purchasing it from the king, in payment of a debt, and from Parliament
c. in payment of a debt, from Parliament, and in return for a favor to the king
d. a, b, and c

2.7 Charters _____ .
a. were issued by Parliament, gave owners authority to govern, and entitled owners to any profits earned
b. gave owners authority to govern, entitled owners to any profits earned, and guaranteed colonists personal rights of Englishmen
c. were issued by Parliament, entitled owners to any profits earned, and guaranteed colonists personal rights of Englishmen
d. were issued by Parliament, gave owners authority to govern, and guaranteed colonists personal rights of Englishmen

2.8 By the mid 1700s, colonies were governed by _____ .
a. governors, governor's council, and assemblies
b. governor's council, assemblies, and companies
c. governors, assemblies, and companies
d. neither a, b, nor c
e. a, b, and c

Complete each activity.

2.9 What kind of people became colonists in America, and for what reasons did they leave their homeland?

_____

_____

_____

_____

_____

2.10 List the restrictions England put on her American colonies in trading.

_____

_____

_____

_____

_____

2.11 How did the colonists react to the trade acts?

_____

_____

_____

_____

_____

Training of war. In addition to the colonies' problems with the mother country, France posed a great threat to the young colonies. With easy access to the center of North America by the St. Lawrence River and the Great Lakes, the French were an imposing shadow looming over the English settlers. As Englishmen tried to expand westward, their advance was checked not only by the Appalachian Mountains, but also by harassment from the French who controlled the western water routes. The French and Indian War finally resolved the issue of which nation would dominate the American interior.

During the first few years of the war, France won impressive victories. They convinced several of the Native American Nations to fight with them, and this constituted a formidable force against the British. French and Native American raids terrorized colonists of western New York and Pennsylvania. Eventually, however, the tide turned; and, following a series of smaller battles, the French were dealt a most decisive defeat in 1759 at the Battle of Quebec. This final English victory was led by General Wolfe against General Montcalm; both generals were fatally wounded in the battle. The Treaty of Paris, signed in 1763, gave England the control of Canada and all the land east of the Mississippi River. Britain also received Florida from Spain. The colonies no longer had to fear France, but their hostilities with England were only just beginning.

After putting down a Native American uprising led by the Ottawa chief, Pontiac, in 1763, the English decided it was time to take control of their colonies. The British resented the poor backing they received from the colonists in fighting France. Some colonists joined forces with the English and fought courageously, but a large percentage refused to support the British troops. Although some colonial officers, including a young colonel from Virginia by the name of George Washington, earned an impressive reputation in battle, such examples were too

few in the minds of English authorities. Each colony had remained separate, using its troops, or **militia**, only within the borders of the state. Colonial governments had resisted giving up their people or money to pay for war expenses. Colonial governments continued to trade with the French during the war, a clear act of treason to the British.

Because of the large debt caused by the war, Great Britain had to tax her own people quite heavily. The British believed that the colonists should also share in paying off the war debts.

King George III ascended the English throne in 1760. Being born and educated in England, the new king had no intention of being merely a figurehead like his father and grandfather. George III was more actively involved in governing than either of his two predecessors. Wanting to rule in all areas of his empire, King George III insisted the trade laws be followed by the colonists.

Officials in England were also anxious to see the trade laws enforced and revenue increased. Writs of assistance and trials without juries were continued as officials tried to strictly enforce the laws. In addition, further taxes were levied on colonists to pay British officials and the British army in the colonies.

One of the taxes was the highly controversial Stamp Act of 1765. The Stamp Act required that British tax stamps be placed on various documents when the tax was paid. Trying to appease the colonists, the English explained that the money would be used in defense of the American colonies. The colonists did not care. Opposition to the Stamp Act was vocal and occasionally violent. The Act was repealed after a year because of the protests.

From the Treaty of Paris (1763) until 1776, hostilities between the British government and the colonies continued to increase. England was determined to be obeyed, especially in the payment of taxes and the following of laws.

The colonists were insistent on their own rights, particularly demanding to be recognized as Englishmen. The colonists added their own pressure by boycotting British goods, which caused English businessmen to bring pressure upon Parliament. British officials were treated roughly; some were even tarred and feathered by the furious colonists. Any action taken by the English to punish these uprisings was met with disruption and violence.

The colonies grew increasingly united in their opposition to England. Representatives of the colonies met together in 1765 to discuss the Stamp Act. In 1774, the first official meeting of the colonial representatives occurred, the First Continental Congress. Although many colonists still thought of themselves as Englishmen, they did not want their lives dictated by a government in Europe that knew nothing of their lives and needs. Many were determined to make a stand for the rights they believed were theirs.

On December 16, 1773, an incident took place in Boston that was a major step leading to war with Britain. That night, colonists, disguised as Native American men, boarded a British ship in Boston harbor and dumped 342 chests of tea into the sea to protest the tax on it. In retaliation, Boston harbor was closed by the British and the city was placed under military rule. Other American colonies rallied behind Boston and sent needed supplies. On September 5, 1774, the First Continental Congress met in Philadelphia to consider the grave situation between the colonies and Great Britain. The stage was set for one of the most dramatic scenes in our nation's history, the Revolutionary War.

| Boston Tea Party

✎   Complete the following sentences.

2.12 In the French and Indian War, the a. _____ and b. _____

fought against the c. _____ and d. _____ .

2.13 The English victory at Quebec was led by a. _____ against

b. _____ .

2.14 The Treaty of Paris gave England control of a. _____ and b. _____

_____ .

2.15 King George III demanded that the colonies obey the _____ .

2.16 The Stamp Act placed taxes on various documents, saying the taxes would be used for

_____ .

2.17 The first official meeting of all colonies was called the _____ .

2.18 A major step towards war with England was the _____ .

Answer the following questions.

2.19 Why were the French a threat to young America?

_____

_____

_____

2.20 Why were American colonists accused of poor backing in the French and Indian War?

_____

_____

_____

2.21 You are an American Patriot involved in the Boston Tea Party. What factors drove you to
your involvement in such a rebellious action against the crown?

_____

_____

_____

_____

_____

_____

AMERICAN FRONTIER

The thirteen colonies eventually came to the point of no return. Attempts to remain loyal to England failed, and war appeared to be the only solution. The Second Continental Congress met after the battle of Lexington and Concord and appointed George Washington commander of the colonial army. In 1776, the congress also drafted a document declaring the independence of the colonies from England. When the war for independence had ended, the people of the colonies would be faced with the task of establishing a foundation for a new nation. The Constitution would be written and ratified, thus becoming the framework for our government.

Establishing a nation. The First Continental Congress tried to reaffirm their position as loyal Englishmen, petitioning their king for redress of their grievances. However, conditions did not improve. Soon, many colonial leaders began speaking of a revolt, including Patrick Henry of Virginia, who stirringly demanded, "Is life so dear, or peace so sweet, as to be purchased at the price of chains and slavery?" Continuing, Henry proclaimed one of the most quoted statements in American history, "Give me liberty or give me death!" In his famous pamphlet entitled *Common Sense*, Thomas Paine recorded his explanation for breaking away from England. In it he made the point that, "It is only common sense that a continent should not be governed by a small island."

In 1774 and 1775 military forces were being built up on both sides. General Thomas Gage, Commander of English forces in America, brought an increasing number of British troops to Massachusetts. Meanwhile, colonial militia began training for future hostilities. Being on the alert to fight at a moment's notice, the forces took on the nickname of *minutemen*. Seizing and destroying military supplies and property, both sides engaged in harassing measures.

| Minutemen statue

On April 18, 1775, General Gage led a force of British soldiers to Lexington, Massachusetts, just outside of Boston, in an effort to seize war supplies stored there. He also hoped to arrest the colonial leaders Samuel Adams and John Hancock. The colonists, however, were warned by fast riders from Boston, including Paul Revere, who was stopped before he could reach Lexington.

When the English force reached Lexington at dawn, approximately seventy-five minutemen were on hand to greet them. When an advance British force challenged them, a shot was fired.

No one knows for sure which side fired that "shot heard 'round the world!" British troops charged, uncontrolled, into the colonial militiamen, leaving eight minutemen dead and ten wounded, with only one English soldier dead. Moving on to Concord, the British killed two Americans while losing three of their own men. As the English troops returned from Concord, they were fired upon by the infuriated militiamen who used every possible means of concealment. The British followed traditional military procedure and marched in file down the main road. This resulted in nearly two hundred British soldiers being killed or wounded during the return march to Boston.

In May of 1775, the Second Continental Congress convened in Philadelphia's Carpenter's Hall. They decided the time for negotiations and petitions was passed. George Washington was appointed Commander-in-Chief of the Continental Army that was quartered around Boston. A committee of five, consisting of Thomas Jefferson from Virginia, Benjamin Franklin from Pennsylvania, John Adams from Massachusetts, Robert Livingston from New York, and Roger Sherman from Connecticut, was appointed to prepare the draft of a declaration of independence from England.

On July 4, 1776, the Declaration of Independence was passed and signed, causing celebration everywhere. Church bells rang and parades were formed as jubilation spread over the spirited colonies. This "birth certificate" of our nation declared the colonies were independent of England and would, henceforth, stand alone under God.

The boldness of this small group of colonies to stand up against one of the world's most powerful nations was remarkable. The nations of Europe sincerely doubted their chances of success. The decision for independence would become a harrowing test of survival for the colonists, one that would be watched skeptically by the rest of the world.

| Signing the Declaration of Independence

Actually, all colonists did not share in the boldness of America's activities in the 1770s. Scholars have estimated that as many as one-third of the colonists remained loyal to England, strongly resisting the idea of independence. Included in this group were many wealthy and powerful businessmen, lawyers, clergymen, and doctors. Those colonists fighting for the English were labeled as Tories, a term of abuse. Some colonists fled from the conflict and returned to England. Approximately one-third of the colonists were neutral and took no active part. The final third of the colonists actively supported independence and were willing to support their beliefs by joining the military or by financing the war supplies.

The colonists were fighting one of the largest and best equipped armies of their time. England also had an excellent navy to move, supply, and support her army. The Tories provided troops, money, and information for the British on American soil. The colonists had only poorly trained and supplied militias to fight the English professionals.

However, the colonists had the obvious advantage of fighting on home soil. The English had the distinct disadvantage of fighting far from home. They had to bring most of their equipment and supplies across the Atlantic Ocean. In addition, many people in England did not like the idea of killing fellow Englishmen and did not want the king's power increased by a victory. Many British people were sympathetic toward the colonists' demands. This opposition necessitated the hiring of Hessians (German soldiers) to fight in the Revolutionary War. Internationally, Holland, Spain, and France gave the colonies much needed support throughout the struggle. English leadership was inept and English generals were poor commanders. Finally, George Washington, commander of the Continental army provided important leadership to the colonies and helped ensure a colonial victory over the British.

At sea, the colonists were greatly outnumbered; British blockades and troop movements were almost impossible to challenge. The most exciting colonial victory of the war on the seas occurred in 1779 when the American ship, *Bonhomme Richard*, commanded by John Paul Jones, captured the English ship, *Seraphis*. At one point in the battle, the British commander asked Jones if he wanted to surrender, to which Jones replied, "I have not yet begun to fight."

On the land the British were better organized and equipped than the colonists. Unfortunately for the American cause, some colonial troops were forbidden by their leaders to fight outside their state border. An additional disadvantage was that the Second Continental Congress had little power of its own. The Continental Congress had to request or borrow money from states to support the war effort because it was not allowed to levy taxes.

The Continental army was at first composed mostly of state militia, who had little organized training. These men would often return home following their short enlistment commitment.

| General Washington in winter

Eventually, volunteers were recruited for longer periods of enlistment.

The colonists were met by a series of defeats or draws during the first months of the war. By December, 1776, the plight of the Washington-led colonial army seemed hopeless. Badly beaten, poorly supplied, and greatly outnumbered, the brave band miraculously held on during this desperate time. The enlistments of many of his soldiers were due to run out with the New Year. Washington needed some way to encourage them to stay.

Thomas Paine wrote of this, "These are the times that try men's souls. The summer soldier and the sunshine patriot will in this crisis shrink from the service of their country; but he that stands it now, deserves the love and thanks of man and woman."

Fortunately for the colonial soldiers, the British decided to observe the European tradition of discontinuing military offensives during the winter months. Heartened by this tradition and in desperate need of a military victory, Washington made a daring move. He led his battered crew in a surprise attack across the Delaware River at night and captured about one thousand British and Hessian troops in Trenton, New Jersey. Although a difficult winter lay ahead, followed by more harsh years of war, the Continental army had won a victory that encouraged them despite desperate circumstances in which they found themselves.

Several more British victories the following year failed in their main purpose to destroy the colonial army and end the revolt. Washington's army continued to survive even during the horrible winter of 1777-78 in Valley Forge, Pennsylvania, when the men faced starvation and painful cold without proper clothing. Moreover, the tide was turning. The Americans won a decisive battle at Saratoga in October of 1777. The victory convinced the French that the colonists could win and they began to openly aid the American cause.

| Commander Cornwallis surrendering

After an eight-year-long struggle, the decisive colonial victory was achieved at Yorktown, Virginia. With the help of a French blockade at sea, and French troops, the colonists forced the British General Cornwallis to surrender his army in 1781. Weary of the economically draining war in which her military leaders committed blunder after blunder, England agreed to negotiate. After six months, a peace treaty was finally signed in Paris in 1783, ending the hostilities and entitling the colonies to the independence for which they had so courageously fought.

Answer true or false.

2.22 _____ Patrick Henry and Thomas Paine were famous colonial patriot leaders.

2.23 _____ Cornwallis's attack on Lexington and Concord sparked the Revolutionary War.

2.24 _____ George Washington was chosen by the First Continental Congress to lead the Continental army.

2.25 _____ The Declaration of Independence, America's "birth certificate," was signed on July 4, 1776.

2.26 _____ John Paul Jones led an exciting colonial sea victory by capturing the *Seraphis*.

2.27 _____ Colonial soldiers spent a bitter winter at Valley Forge.

2.28 _____ Cornwallis's surrender at Yorktown was a combined effort of colonists on land and Spanish at sea.

2.29 _____ The 1781 Treaty of Paris ended the hostilities, giving the colonists their independence.

Complete the following activities.

2.30 Fill in the American and British advantages and disadvantages in the Revolutionary War.

AMERICA		ENGLAND	
ADVANTAGES	**DISADVANTAGES**	**ADVANTAGES**	**DISADVANTAGES**

2.31 Write the answers to each question concerning winter warfare.

a. Why didn't England fight during the winter?

_____

_____

_____

b. What advantage did this custom give Americans?

_____

_____

_____

c. What did the Trenton victory do for American troops?

_____

_____

_____

2.32 You are an American colonist in the 1770s. Where do your sentiments lie—are you a Tory, neutral, or a Patriot? Give good arguments to back up your position, and hand them, written, to your teacher, who will pick the best papers for a debate. Be clear and strong in your arguments.

TEACHER CHECK _____ _____

initials   date

2.33 Complete the chart about colonial victories and defeats during the Revolutionary War. You should use an encyclopedia or some other source.

AMERICAN VICTORIES AND DEFEATS					
	LEXINGTON AND CONCORD	RETURN MARCH TO BOSTON	BATTLE OF TRENTON	SEIZURE OF SERAPHIS	BATTLE OF YORKTOWN
a. American Commander					
b. British Commander					
c. American Strategy					
d. British Strategy					
e. Victor					
f. Significance					

HISTORY & GEOGRAPHY 1006

LIFEPAC TEST

NAME _____

DATE _____

SCORE _____

HISTORY & GEOGRAPHY 1006: LIFEPAC TEST

Match the following items (each answer, 2 points).

1. _____ Oliver Cromwell
2. _____ Cavaliers
3. _____ George Washington
4. _____ coup d' état
5. _____ Code Napoleon
6. _____ Bastille Day
7. _____ Articles of Confederation
8. _____ Robert Walpole
9. _____ Tories
10. _____ writs of assistance
11. _____ Treaty of Paris (1763)
12. _____ Voltaire
13. _____ Cornwallis
14. _____ Declaration of the Rights of Man
15. _____ Danton

a. sudden seizure of power
b. French Independence Day
c. search warrants
d. supporters of Charles I
e. famous French writer
f. wanted strong English king under Charles II
g. gave England control of Canada
h. leader of Roundheads
i. leader of the Jacobin Club
j. first American constitution
k. surrendered at Yorktown
l. first British prime minister
m. commander of colonial army
n. military dictator of France
o. personal freedoms for the French
p. French laws organized by Napoleon

Complete the following sentences (each answer, 4 points).

16. The two branches of Parliament include a. _____ and b. _____ .

17. The leader of the English Parliament is called the _____ .

18. The three branches of the government of the United States are a. _____ , b. _____ , and c. _____ .

19. France's estates included the a. _____ , b. _____ , and c. _____ .

20. The National Assembly's vow to write a constitution was called the _____ _____ .

Write the letter for the correct answer on the line (each answer, 2 points).

21. Government by one ruler is called a _____ .
a. monarchy   b. democracy   c. parliamentary   d. socialist

22. British naval power soared in respect after the defeat of _____ .
a. James II   b. Cornwallis
c. the Spanish Armada   d. George Washington

23. The English Revolution put _____ in control of British affairs.
a. the House of Lords   b. Congress
c. Parliament   d. the Directory

24. The Church of England was established under _____ .
a. Henry VI   b. James I   c. Charles II   d. Henry VIII

25. The Habeas Corpus Act assured a person of a trial within _____ .
a. six months   b. twenty days   c. fifty days   d. one year

26. When Charles I sent troops into the House of Commons, this action lead to the outbreak of the _____ .
a. War of Roses   b. French and Indian War
c. English Bill of Rights   d. English Revolution

27. Parliament had very limited power under the _____ .
a. Stuarts   b. Tudors   c. Hapsburgs

28. The branch of the English Parliament composed of the clergy and selected nobles is the

_____ .
a. House of Lords   b. House of Commons
c. Senate   d. House of Representatives

29. The final battle of the French and Indian War was the _____ .
a. Battle of Lexington   b. Battle of Waterloo
c. Battle of Quebec   d. Battle of Yorktown

30. The president of the United States is elected by the _____ .
a. electoral college   b. House of Representatives
c. people   d. a, b, and c

Answer true or false (each answer, 1 point).

31. _____ Napoleon conquered Russia on two occasions.

32. _____ General Gage was the British commander at the Battle of Lexington.

33. _____ Amendments and the balance of power are strong points of the United States Constitution.

34. _____ The Separatists and the Puritans were groups of Presbyterians.

35. _____ French writers and the American Revolution inspired the French to move toward their own revolution.

36. _____ The Consulate brought weak, unorganized leadership to France.

37. _____ Napoleon made great reforms in French banking, education, and law.

38. _____ The invasion of Austria brought the start of defeat to Napoleon.

39. _____ The Revolutions in England, the United States, and France gave people more voice in their government.

40. _____ The Boston Tea Party was a revolt against English taxes.

Building the foundation. During the years of the Revolutionary War, the colonies had little government. The second Continental Congress did not organize any centralized power until six months before Cornwallis' surrender at Yorktown. At that time, all the states had approved a constitution they hoped would provide the basis for a strong central government.

The Articles of Confederation, the name of our first constitution, established a Congress which contained one house and gave a vote to each state. Congress was given the authority to make war, peace, borrow money, and settle any arguments between states. It did not have the power to tax, however. Laws made by Congress had to be enforced by individual states as they wished.

This first constitution of the United States was really too weak to work well. After being in effect from 1781 to 1788, a new constitution, developed in 1787 and adopted in 1788, replaced it. George Washington became the first president of the United States under the new Constitutional government.

This new Constitution has continued in effect until the present day, a testimony to its flexibility and applicability to changing situations of the nation and its people. Whereas the Constitution has guided the United States for over 200 years, the Word of God has guided men throughout history. The psalmist wrote (Psalm 119:89), "Forever, O LORD, thy word is settled in heaven." Also, Jesus said (Matthew 24:35), "Heaven and earth shall pass away, but my words shall not pass away." God's Word is permanent, a sure source of wisdom and guidance for life.

The new Constitution created a central government that was firm enough to force states to act together when necessary. However, enough freedom was given to the states to deal with their individual problems without interference from the central government. At times both state and national governments were permitted to work together.

Under the new Constitution three branches of government were created. The *executive* branch, the president and vice president, are elected by an electoral college system. Electors are chosen by the people, who, in turn, choose the president. Traditionally the electors vote for the candidate selected by the political party to which they belong. A popular vote decides which electors and their candidate will be chosen. The position of president is both awesome and powerful. The president is not only a national leader, but also an international leader. The **legislative** branch, the Congress, has the authority to make laws for the United States. The Constitution provides for two houses in Congress, the House of Representatives and the Senate, staffed with representatives chosen by the people. The **judicial** branch, the courts of the United States, has the responsibility of interpreting the laws and evaluating how they apply to various situations. Today, the United States has three levels of courts: district courts, courts of appeal, and the Supreme Court.

One of the strong points of our Constitution is its flexibility. Our federal government's branches overlap and share responsibilities to a certain degree. Each branch's duty to the American people is clearly defined and executed. What this means is that the president of the United States will not be arriving at the door of every fire and police emergency in the country, nor will a firefighter enact any new law. The firefighter may at any time write to his state's representatives, and even the president, to suggest changes. The Constitution can be amended to meet the various needs of the people. The first ten amendments are known as the Bill of Rights.

The United States government also contains an automatic checking system for the three branches of government, creating a healthy balance of power between them. The central government, known as the Federal government, has the authority to do things states cannot do individually, such as declaring war and printing money. However, both central and state governments are prohibited from infringing upon or taking away individual citizen rights, rights basic to the freedom we prize so dearly in the United States.

The Constitution has served our country well for over two hundred years. This stability can be attributed to a number of its vital qualities. First, the Constitution was designed to meet the needs of the people. Secondly, its strength lies in its ability to separate the various power groups—executive, legislative, and judicial—and hold them in balance. Finally, the Constitution has been flexible in meeting the changes our country has experienced in the past two hundred years. Being such a young nation, we need to thank God for providing men with the great wisdom and foresight needed to draw up such a valuable framework for our government.

In an amazingly short amount of time, the young American frontier came of age. No longer a struggling group of colonies under the shackles of a foreign monarch, the United States of America stood on her own feet, a free republic under God.

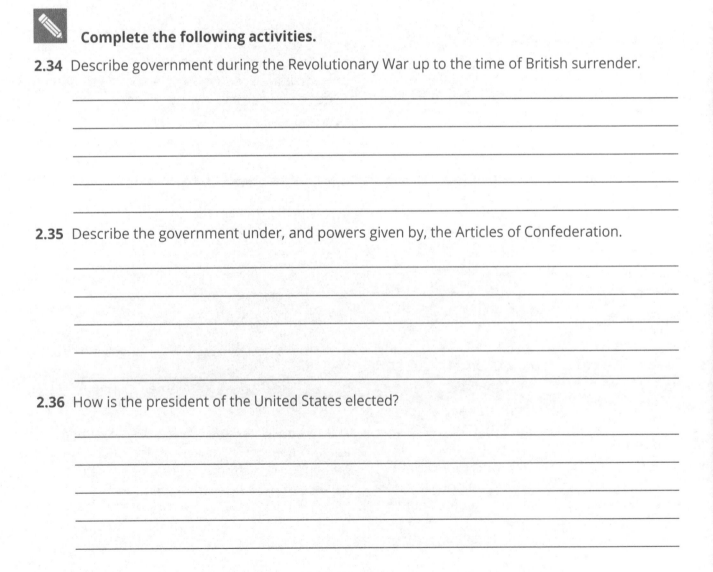

Complete the following activities.

2.34 Describe government during the Revolutionary War up to the time of British surrender.

_____

_____

_____

_____

_____

2.35 Describe the government under, and powers given by, the Articles of Confederation.

_____

_____

_____

_____

2.36 How is the president of the United States elected?

_____

_____

_____

_____

_____

2.37 Fill in the following chart on the American government under the new Constitution, giving its branches and their levels or divisions.

GOVERNMENT OF THE UNITED STATES OF AMERICA		
EXECUTIVE	**LEGISLATIVE**	**JUDICIAL**
Power		
Divisions		

2.38 As the creator of the new Constitution of 1788, you are chosen to present its strengths as compared to the previous constitution's weaknesses. What areas of importance will you stress in attempting to get it passed unanimously?

_____

_____

_____

_____

2.39 Chart the laws, acts, and taxes placed by England on colonial America that led to the revolt of the colonies.

TEACHER CHECK _____ _____
                                                   initials   date

Review the material in this section in preparation for the Self Test. This Self Test will check your mastery of this particular section as well as your knowledge of the previous section.

SELF TEST 2

Identify the following names and terms (each answer, 3 points).

2.01   Parliament _____

_____

2.02   divine right _____

_____

2.03   Oliver Cromwell _____

_____

2.04   English trade acts _____

_____

2.05   Stamp Act _____

_____

Give the significance of the following battles (each answer, 3 points).

2.06   Battle of Quebec _____

_____

_____

2.07   Battle of Lexington and Concord _____

_____

_____

2.08   Battle of Trenton _____

_____

_____

2.09   Battle of Yorktown _____

_____

_____

2.010   Capture of the *Seraphis* _____

_____

_____

Complete the following sentences (each answer, 3 points).

2.011   The English Revolution put _____ in control of British affairs rather than the king.

2.012   Presbyterians and Puritans were both religious followers of _____

_____ .

2.013   Two bills bringing personal liberties to Englishmen were the a. _____

and b. _____ .

2.014   Colonists were guaranteed treatment as a. _____

by the royal b. _____ .

2.015   By the mid 1700s, government in the colonies included a governor, a. _____

_____ , and a(n) b. _____ .

2.016   The doctrine that teaches that a colony should support the mother country with raw

materials and goods is called _____ .

2.017   The French and Indian War was mainly fought between the a. _____

and b. _____ .

2.018   The Articles of Confederation was the first United States _____ .

2.019   Branches of the government of the United States, aside from the executive branch, were

the a. _____ and b. _____ branches.

2.020   Congress is divided into two houses: a. _____

and b. _____ .

Answer true or false (each answer, 1 point).

2.021   _____   The Cavaliers and Roundheads were England's political parties under Charles II.

2.022   _____   Cavaliers and Tories supported the rule of the king.

2.023   _____   Writs of assistance allowed the English to search anywhere in the colonies at anytime.

2.024   _____   Colonists believed that their rights as Englishmen were being abused by the Bill of Rights.

2.025   _____   The 1763 Treaty of Paris gave England control of Canada and all the land east of the Mississippi River.

2.026   _____   The First Continental Congress was the first governing body in America.

2.027   _____   The Battle of Quebec gave Washington's troops the incentive they needed to overcome the hardships of winter.

2.028 _____ The president of the United States is elected by the electoral college system.

2.029 _____ The legislative branch of our government makes and enforces the laws of our country.

2.030 _____ Amendments to the Constitution allow for necessary changes through time.

Answer the following questions (each answer, 4 points).

2.031 What different ways were American colonies founded, and how was land in America received?

_____

_____

_____

_____

2.032 How did the French and Indian War help America?

_____

_____

_____

_____

2.033 What were the advantages and disadvantages of the colonies during the Revolutionary War?

a. advantages _____

_____

_____

b. disadvantages _____

_____

_____

Complete this chart (each answer, 2 points).

2.034 Compare English and American governments in these areas after their revolutions.

	ENGLAND	AMERICA
Head of government		
Lawmaking body		
Houses of lawmaking body		
Enforcer of laws		
How government head is chosen		
How government head is replaced		
Personal freedoms listed in		

106/132 **SCORE** _____ **TEACHER** _____ _____
initials   date

3. FRENCH REVOLUTION

France, inspired by the victories in England and America, became the third Western nation to experience a large-scale revolution. The Old Regime with all its culture, splendor, and surface prosperity was ready to collapse. A new leadership from outside the old **aristocracy** was growing in France.

The ten years between 1789 and 1799 was a time of struggle and violence in France. The French Revolution began when Louis XVI called the **Estates**-General to provide money for his bankrupt government. The French Revolution ended when Napoleon Bonaparte became first consul of France. During the ten years of the French Revolution, thousands of aristocrats, including the king and queen, lost their lives on the **guillotine**.

At the beginning of the Revolution, the king held supreme power in France. By the end of the Revolution, this power had passed to the hands of the large, growing middle class. The Bourbon kings returned to the throne in 1814 and 1815, after each defeat of Napoleon. However, their absolute power was gone forever in France. The Revolution did not make France a democracy; however, it did make France an unstable, limited monarchy.

In this section you will examine the factors which led to the unrest of the people in France and learn about the measures taken by the National Assembly to bring stability to France. You will also study the rise of the National Convention, the Directory, and Napoleon. The positive actions of reform taken by Napoleon in France, and his attempts to conquer Europe, will also be examined.

Section Objectives

Review these objectives. When you have completed this section, you should be able to:

13. Describe the factors during the reigns of Louis XV and Louis XVI which led to the people's unrest against the Old Regime and the onset of the French Revolution.

14. Describe the measures taken by the National Assembly and the reasons for its fall.

15. Explain the steps taken by the National Convention and the government of its Directory.

16. Describe the steps leading to the takeover of France by Napoleon and government under his Consulate.

17. Describe Napoleon's positive actions of reform in France.

18. Describe Napoleon's offensive for control of Europe and the steps leading to his downfall and final defeat.

Vocabulary

Study these words to enhance your learning success in this section.

absolutism	aristocracy	coalition
conscription	coup d'état	émigrés'
estates	guillotine	lettres de cachet
nationalism		

OLD REGIME

The violations of human rights and individual freedoms that led to revolutions in both England and the American colonies also existed in France. Between the 1500s and the 1700s, France had grown into a strong, powerful nation. The kings and their ministers also became powerful. The French king's authority became absolute. The premier example of the age of **absolutism** was Louis XIV of France. When his prime minister died in 1661, Louis decided that he would rule personally without a prime minister. France suffered from a series of expensive wars and an extraordinarily expensive royal court under Louis. The construction of public buildings, such as the palace at Versailles, added an additional financial burden to the debt of the French people.

During the reign of Louis XV and Louis XVI, the people became more dissatisfied. By the late 1700s discontent swept through France like a fire. The government was bankrupt, and Louis XVI was too weak to handle the situation. In 1789 the people's discontent led to the French Revolution, which lasted for ten years.

Louis XV. Headed by Louis XV, an absolute monarch who reigned from 1715 to 1774, France's troubles steadily mounted under the king's lazy and indifferent attitude toward the needs of the French people. The French were divided into three classes, or **estates**: the clergy, the nobles, and everyone else (middle class and peasants). Although the last estate did most of the work and paid most of the taxes, they received few benefits.

God-given rights, so clearly defended in the Constitution of the United States, did not exist in France under the troubled monarchy. True personal liberty did not exist within the French system. Freedom of speech, the press, and preference of worship were absent in France. As in the colonies under King George III, judges were appointed and removed by the king. The few trials that were conducted were held

secretly and without a jury. Often, sentencing was done by the king's decree, in **lettres de cachet**, without the benefit of any trial at all. Many unfortunate victims were held in French prisons, including the famous Bastille in Paris, without even knowing why they were imprisoned.

Influenced by the English and American revolutions (especially the latter), attacks against France's Old Regime's traditions and beliefs steadily grew stronger. Such attacks first came from famous French writers, such as Voltaire, Rousseau, and Montesquieu. These writers specifically targeted the absolute rule of the French monarchs (by divine right), unfair taxes, and the special privileges held by the nobility. The Roman Catholic Church was also strongly criticized because of its vast land holdings, the wealth it possessed, the money it collected from the people, and the tight control it had over education.

France also had the burden of a tremendous debt amassed through wars and the poor financial policies of former French governments. The French Court devoured great quantities of money with the lavish life style of the nobility. Although prosperous as a country, France had difficulty meeting its public expenses even with an excessive tax load on the middle and peasant classes.

The difficulty in meeting financial commitments could have been greatly relieved had France's wealthy citizens been willing to pay their fair share of the taxes. But, longstanding French laws exempted both the clergy and the nobility from taxation. Because the wealthiest citizens were not paying, taxes continually increased, driving businesses steadily downward as their owners became less able to meet their tax payments. Of course, the greatest injustice fell upon the peasant class who had the most difficulty meeting the tax burden. Faced with this problem of meeting the country's expenses,

Louis XV borrowed more and more from bankers. As Louis continued to borrow, he cared little that France grew financially and economically weaker.

The financial situation, however, was not the only factor motivating the middle and peasant classes in their disdain of the French monarchial government. The success of the American Revolution strongly influenced them as well. The quality of man and his right to determine his own destiny by self-government made a lasting impression on the minds of many Frenchmen. The fact that the United States had been able to break the grip of a king who did not have the people's best interests at heart was especially inspiring to the French who longed for a government by the people.

Because of the indolence of Louis XV, the Old Regime totally ignored the dissension growing among the people. What Louis XV would not do, his grandson and successor from 1774 to 1792, Louis XVI, could not do.

 **Complete the following sentences.**

3.1 The three estates of France were a. _____ ,

b. _____ , and the c. _____ .

3.2 Three French writers who attacked the Old Regime were a. _____ ,

b. _____ , and c. _____ .

3.3 Three factors of the American Revolution that inspired the French were

a. _____ ,

b. _____ ,

and c. _____ .

Answer the following questions.

3.4 What kind of king was Louis XV of France, and why did he not take any steps to avoid the coming revolution?

_____

_____

_____

_____

3.5 What factors during the reign of Louis XV hastened the coming of the French Revolution?

_____

_____

_____

_____

3.6 You are a member of the third estate during France's Old Regime. What do you dislike or think unfair in your government that which is leading to your continued unrest?

_____

_____

_____

_____

_____

_____

_____

_____

_____

_____

TEACHER CHECK _____ _____

initials   date

Louis XVI. Louis XVI became king at the age of nineteen. Having received the news that his grandfather had passed away leaving him to be king, Louis exclaimed, "What a burden! At my age! And I have been taught nothing!" Although the new king had the reputation of being sincere and honest, he was also known to be stubborn and hesitant in making decisions. His wife, Marie Antoinette, was one of sixteen children and a member of the famous Hapsburg family of Austria. Never popular with the French people, Marie Antoinette reminded many citizens of the unpopular alliance between France and Austria during Europe's Seven Years' War. She lost more favor with the common people of France when the royal court received the report that many of them were starving because of a shortage of bread, and she was quoted (possibly misquoted) to have said, "Let them eat cake! " Eventually, Marie Antoinette was sent to the French **guillotine** where she was beheaded.

Actually, Louis XVI would not have been considered a poor ruler during normal times, but the late 1700s could not be deemed ordinary times in France. The Age of Revolution definitely was not the time for a monarch who lacked strength. With a treasury nearing bankruptcy and a people being repeatedly abused by negligent and unfair leaders, Louis XVI was facing an inevitable revolt. Although Louis XVI made some effort to prevent the collapse of the French monarchy, it was too late to keep his country from disaster.

In a desperate and final attempt to reform the government, Louis XVI put forth a plan he hoped would be successful in halting the critical economic slide. Financial experts, called by the king to suggest economic improvements, listed three major things that needed to be done: (1) give greater freedom and encouragement to French industry, (2) cut down on lavish spending by the king's court, and (3) require nobles and the clergy to pay taxes.

| Marie Antoinette

When these proposals were rejected by the king's court and especially the extravagant Marie Antoinette, France's last chance to avoid a revolution faded from view. Financial disaster was imminent when bankers refused to continue lending money to the troubled French government. Thus, in 1789, the king was forced to call representatives of the people together; this was the spark for the French Revolution.

The meeting of these representatives was the resurrection of the former French legislative body known as the Estates-General. They met to consider the country's financial problems, business depression, and growing unemployment. All three classes were represented in their traditional groups: clergy, nobles, and everyone else.

The king tried to persuade the estates to meet in their three separate groups and vote on issues by estates. That would have given the third estate, with most of the population, only one out of three votes on decisions. The third estate vehemently refused, demanding that all the estates meet together and form a National Assembly. The king and the other estates refused. Therefore, the third estate declared itself a National Assembly. Countering this move, the king barred the third estate from the meeting. They then met at a tennis court, where they vowed in the Oath of the Tennis Court to write a constitution that would be accepted by France. The king relented and allowed the third estate to return. Representatives of the first and second estates joined together with the third to form an assembly in which each representative had a vote. This was the birth of the National Assembly.

Shortly after the confrontation with the third estate, Louis XVI blundered again. He began bringing soldiers into Paris and Versailles, where the representatives were meeting. This move caused the restless people of Paris to riot on July 14, 1789, resulting in the capture of the Bastille, the hated royal political prison. Bastille Day is still celebrated in France as their Independence Day. A new government was set up in the city of Paris; and a people's army, the *National Guard*, was formed under the command of General Lafayette, who had acquired his fame as a hero in the successful American Revolution.

The Paris riots soon spread to the countryside. Frustrated peasants overran and destroyed monasteries, wealthy mansions, and government property, killing many nobles and government officials in the violent uprisings. In an attempt to restore order and discipline, the Assembly abolished the feudal system of serfdom and peasant services that had survived since the Middle Ages. The National Assembly also adopted the Declaration of the Rights of Man. Beginning by declaring freedom of speech, the press, and religion, the declaration

| Storming of the Bastille

went on to say that men were not only born equal and should remain so before the law, but were also entitled to the rights of self-government, personal liberty, and fair trials.

Dealing with the nobility, however, was extremely difficult. Many fled France to neighboring countries, vowing to return someday and regain control. Others of the **aristocracy** convinced Louis XVI to call troops to Versailles in support of their cause and to disband the Assembly. This decision brought more violence.

On October 5, 1789, several thousand women and some men marched on Versailles from Paris. After demanding food from the National Assembly and the king, the crowd forced the king and his royal family to move to Paris. The National Assembly also moved to Paris, realizing how much they were at the mercy of the Paris mobs.

By 1791 the National Assembly was ready to fulfill its Oath of the Tennis Court by completing its constitution. Contained within its pages was the provision for a limited monarchy with separate executive, legislative, and judicial branches. The king's powers were greatly limited, giving him no power to proclaim laws himself. The legislature had one house, elected by tax-paying voters. Since only property owners could hold office, most of the power was held by the middle class.

The new constitutional monarchy had a short-lived existence due to pressures at home and abroad. Nobles who had emigrated to foreign countries (**émigrés**) tried to get support in resisting the new government. They dealt secretly with Louis XVI and eventually persuaded him to flee the country. While trying to escape, however, Louis, his wife, and his children were caught and returned. The hatred and suspicion of the people grew and the revolution became increasingly violent.

The only legislative assembly elected under the new constitution began on October 1, 1791. It immediately faced a crucial test from foreign soldiers. A group of European countries joined to form an army to invade France and to stamp out the dangerous growing spirit of revolution. In retaliation, Louis XVI was forced to sign a declaration of war against Austria and Prussia. This touched off mob violence once again in Paris, bringing additional pressure against the Assembly to rid France of the king's office.

The constitutional monarchy crumbled, bringing about a complete change of government in the middle of a war. Louis XVI and his family were placed in prison. The assembly was disbanded and newly elected National Convention met to lead the country and write another constitution. Lafayette left as commander of the army and joined the émigrés'. Georges Jacques Danton, Maximilien Robespierre, and Jean Paul Marat led a group that seized control of the Paris city government and the government of France.

The pressure of Austrian and Prussian invaders meant that the very survival of the new government was in doubt. The fearful and oppressive atmosphere led to the darkest days of the revolution, the Reign of Terror.

Write the letter for the correct answer on each line.

3.7 Troubles facing Louis XVI's rule were _____ .

  a. unpopular wife, near bankrupt treasury, hesitancy in making decisions, and English harassment

  b. near bankrupt treasury, hesitancy in making decisions, people's unrest from poor leaders, and English harassment

  c. unpopular wife, near bankrupt treasury, hesitancy in making decisions, and people's unrest from poor leaders

  d. unpopular wife, near bankrupt treasury, people's unrest from poor leaders, and English harassment

3.8 Suggestions that financial experts gave to France were to _____ .

  a. encourage industry, raise third estate taxes, and require wealthy to pay taxes

  b. encourage industry, cut down royal spending, and require wealthy to pay taxes

  c. raise third estate taxes, cut down royal spending, and require wealthy to pay taxes

  d. a, b, and c

3.9 Measures taken by the National Assembly include _____ .

  a. made Danton ruler of France, abolished feudal system, and adopted Declaration of the Rights of Man

  b. made Danton ruler of France, adopted Declaration of the Rights of Man, and set up constitutional monarchy

  c. made Danton ruler of France, abolished feudal system, set up constitutional monarchy

  d. abolished feudal system, adopted Declaration of the Rights of Man, and set up constitutional monarchy

3.10 The French Revolution during the reign of Louis XVI included _____ .

  a. rejection of financial improvements, recall of Estates-General, Declaration of the Rights of Man, Bastille Day, and invasion by Austria and Prussia

  b. recall of Estates-General, Declaration of the Rights of Man, invasion of Spain, Bastille Day, invasion by Austria and Prussia, and takeover by Danton

  c. rejection of financial improvements, recall of Estates-General, Declaration of the Rights of Man, invasion of Spain, invasion by Austria and Prussia, and takeover by Danton

  d. a, b, and c

Identify the following.

3.11 Estates-General _____

_____

3.12 National Assembly _____

_____

3.13 Oath of the Tennis Court _____

_____

3.14 Bastille Day _____

_____

3.15 Declaration of the Rights of Man _____

_____

_____

Answer each question.

3.16 What factors necessitated the recall of the Estates-General by Louis XVI?

_____

_____

_____

_____

3.17 What factors brought the birth of the National Assembly?

_____

_____

_____

_____

_____

3.18 Why was the outcome of France's government in such doubt after the takeover by Danton?

_____

_____

_____

_____

_____

NEW LEADERSHIP

Convention successes. Fortunately for the National Convention, its army, led by its new Commander, General Charles Francois Dumouriez, defeated the Austrian and Prussian forces. The National Convention of 1792 greeted this good news by declaring an end to the monarchy and the beginning of a French republic. The National Convention then put Louis XVI on trial for treason. The king was found guilty and sentenced to death. On January 21, 1793, he went to the guillotine where he was publicly beheaded.

Having stopped the invading troops, the French army, under Dumouriez, continued to push onward until they drove the Austrian and Prussian armies out of their country. Following this success in their homeland, they went on to invade the Austrian Netherlands, capturing the city of Brussels. So impressed were they by their army's triumphs, that the National Convention publicly announced their intention of liberating all of Europe from the Old Regime.

The greatest danger to this declaration was the fact that they aimed to achieve their goal by force. As the French Revolution took on an international scope, England, Spain, and Holland joined Austria and Prussia in a **coalition** against the French. Many Frenchmen were also opposed to the tactic of spreading their ideas by the power of gun powder. Following Lafayette's example, Dumouriez gave up the command of his army and joined the opposition.

The French soon faced another invasion. The National Convention met this new crisis by initiating conscription of men into the army. Proving to be a wise decision, the draft gave the army the young men needed to meet the formidable challenge facing them. Led by Lazare Nicolas Carnot, Organizer of Victory, the soldiers brought instant success. The army was now composed of young, loyal, and patriotic men. Unlike previous forces, the officers were representative of all French estates and were well respected by their subordinates.

| The French guillotine

Reign of Terror. While the army was winning victories, the government of France descended to its most barbaric level. Led by Danton's group, the Jacobin Club, the Convention set up the Committee of Public Safety which ruled the country with dictatorial power. The Committee had hundreds of thousands of its opponents, or presumed opponents, jailed. Close to 18,000 people were executed for various "crimes" against the government. Freedom of speech no longer included the right to criticize the government. The leaders of the Jacobin Club eventually began to fight among themselves. Robespierre had Danton executed along with other former leaders. Soon, the people grew weary of the bloodshed. Robespierre himself was condemned and killed in 1794. That marked the end of the Reign of Terror.

The Directory. The European coalition was driven off by 1795; however, victory did not come easily for the French. Not only were many lives lost in the fighting, but the country's treasury was also depleted. The French army had grown dangerously strong and popular, and had crushed any opposition to the National Convention. After the excesses of the Reign of Terror, the Convention wanted a more stable government controlled by the conservative middle class.

The National Convention did pass many helpful reforms. French laws were organized into a code, a national system of public education was set up, slavery was abolished in French colonies, and the metric system of weights and measurements was adopted. Many of these were never put into full effect because of the collapse of the revolution. Yet, even these could not help the unpopularity of the Convention after the Reign of Terror. Another uprising occurred in Paris in 1795. This one, however was quickly smothered by French soldiers led by a young, brilliant officer by the name of Napoleon Bonaparte. This action marked the beginning of his rapid rise to power.

Yet another constitution went into effect in 1795. The constitution restricted voting to property owners, most of whom were middle class. The new executive branch of government, called the Directory, consisted of a committee of five men, called Directors. The legislature made laws and appointed the directors. The Directory ruled France from 1795 to 1799. Its reign was short-lived because it was unable to give France a stable government or a peaceful existence.

The Directory satisfied few people, trying to be a middle-of-the-road government. It was beset by economic problems and continued wars. Both the supporters of the Jacobin Club and the monarchy opposed it. Because they continually argued among themselves, the Directors provided inept and unreliable leadership for the French people.

| Napoleon Bonaparte

This weak leadership left France vulnerable to a military takeover, which had been long feared by many Frenchmen.

Unlike the Directory, the French army had superb leadership. Continued victories against England and Austria gave many military leaders fame and national recognition, with Napoleon Bonaparte standing high above his compatriots. Having previously saved the Convention from Paris mobs, Napoleon already had the government's respect. He used this advantage wisely in his quest for power.

Born in 1769 on the island of Corsica to Italian parents, Napoleon moved to France to attend military school, where he graduated as an artillery officer. Called a military genius by many, Napoleon led France to victories against the Austrians and Sardinians. He became a general at the young age of twenty-six. Short, domineering, and extremely ambitious, Bonaparte was a master organizer and administrator in political and military affairs. Some would argue that this transplanted Corsican was one of the greatest military leaders of history.

Following an especially impressive triumph in Italy, Napoleon returned to France as a national hero. Fearing his popularity, the Directory persuaded Bonaparte to sail with an army to Egypt to disrupt English trade there. This move proved to be a disaster as Napoleon's army met a humiliating defeat in Syria. Bonaparte secretly escaped to France, where he minimized the true situation, even exaggerating his victories previous to the Syrian disaster. With his shining image hardly blemished, the former artillery captain was in the right place at the right time. France was in a state of uncertainty and confusion. An increasing number of Frenchmen were looking for a strong leader who would lead them out of their fear and chaos.

Sensing the timeliness of the hour, Napoleon plotted to seize power by overthrowing the government. Backed by his army and with the strong support of the French people, Bonaparte forced three of the Directors to resign. Arresting the remaining two, he then forced the legislature to dissolve. Later describing the 1799 takeover, Napoleon proudly stated, "I found the crown of France lying on the ground, and I picked it up with a sword."

Napoleon's **coup d'état** gave the French their fourth constitution in ten years. Because its executive branch was made up of three consuls who were appointed for ten years, the new government was known as the Consulate. The true power of the Consulate rested in the office of First Consul, the position to which Napoleon conveniently appointed himself. Along with his command of the army and navy, Napoleon also exercised the power to appoint or dismiss officials and the authority to oppose all new laws.

The legislature, given little if any power, was composed of several assemblies established only as puppets in the hands of the First Consul.

Napoleon modified some of the ideas of the French Revolution. He, too, stressed equality, but explained that liberty meant freedom of opportunity. He taught that people should obey their leader, who in turn ought to govern to the best of his ability for the good of the people. The principles of the Declaration of the Rights of Man continued in effect, and the feudal system remained abolished, allowing peasants to keep their land. All that Napoleon proposed and provided, the French generally agreed to, as long as the peace and security they so desperately sought came along with it.

The Christian can experience peace and security through the Lord Jesus Christ; Isaiah 9:6 relates that Jesus is "...The mighty God, The everlasting Father, The Prince of Peace." Through this Prince we have peace, security, and hope for our lives. The peace that men seek through the governments of the world is not a lasting peace. However, the peace the Christian receives from Jesus Christ endures forever.

Complete the following sentences.

3.19 The military policy strengthening the French army under the National Convention was the

_____ .

3.20 The government established by the constitution of 1795 was called the _____ .

3.21. Napoleon's government was controlled by three _____ .

Complete these activities.

3.22 List the measures that were taken by the National Convention.

_____

_____

_____

_____

_____

_____

_____

3.23 What factors led to the fall of the Directory?

_____

_____

_____

3.24 What were the steps leading to Napoleon's takeover of France?

_____

_____

_____

_____

_____

Complete the following chart.

3.25 Compare and contrast the governments under the Directory and Consulate.

	DIRECTORY	CONSULATE
Executive branch		
Top leader		
Power of top year		
Legislature's power		
Effectiveness		

Complete this writing assignment.

3.26 You are a Frenchman in 1799. What events and traits made you turn to Napoleon as your hope for freedom from the fears and chaos of daily living in France?

_____

_____

_____

_____

_____

TEACHER CHECK _____ _____

initials   date

The Napoleon years. Napoleon's coup d'état on November 9, 1799, made him dictator of France. So great was his influence on the rest of the continent that his years of rule (1799-1814) became known as the Napoleonic Era of Europe. Many neighboring nations were heavily influenced by the French during this period. These nations developed strong feelings of patriotism and loyalty toward their own countries. This movement, developing great pride in one's country and heritage, became known as **nationalism**.

Napoleon's immediate task was to reorganize the French army. He stressed discipline and emphasized strong leadership in his officers. Though the nation still used **conscription** to staff its military, Bonaparte's ability to inspire others developed loyalty and patriotism within the armed forces.

Napoleon set out to defeat France's enemies once his position was secure. He defeated the Austrians in Northern Italy in 1800. The Austrians signed a peace treaty in 1801, ending their war with France. The British drove the French out of Egypt in 1801 and then agreed to negotiate a truce. When a French–English peace agreement was signed in 1802, the French appeared to have attained the peace and security they desired. They were finally at peace after ten long years of war. However, France, Europe, and the rest of the world soon discovered that Napoleon had a much greater desire for power than for peace.

Turning his eyes toward French reforms, Napoleon reorganized the government, initiated economic and social reforms, and reviewed laws started by the National Convention. At the same time, he permitted no criticism or opposition to his measures. Objectors received severe punishments.

A committee of French legal scholars was appointed to review the country's laws. They organized and arranged many and omitted others. Known as the Code Napoleon, this newly formed legal code was widely copied and admired throughout the world.

Napoleon formed the Bank of France to establish a central financial institution. Privately run, but carefully observed by government, it became one of the strongest financial institutions in the world.

The establishment of a French public educational system was also undertaken. Elementary, secondary, and technical schools were founded. The schools emphasized loyalty and obedience to the government and its ruler.

In his consuming passion for world power, respect, and prestige, Napoleon declared France an empire and himself Emperor Napoleon I in 1804. The pope came to Notre Dame Cathedral to crown the new emperor. As the pope proceeded to place the crown on Napoleon's head, Bonaparte grabbed it and put it on himself, signifying that his was the ultimate power.

Dismissing the French desire for peace, Bonaparte set out on a personal quest to dominate Europe. Realizing this quest could never be accomplished without dealing with England, he had begun by declaring war on England in 1803. He initiated a tremendous buildup of the French navy to meet the English on the ocean. To Napoleon's great dismay, a British fleet, under the command of Admiral Horatio Nelson defeated and practically destroyed the combined Spanish and French fleet off Cape Trafalgar in 1805.

Next, Napoleon tried to blockade England from trading with the other nations of Europe. Britain responded to this by doing the same to France. Although Great Britain remained a constant thorn to the French, supporting any who would oppose Napoleon, the rest of Europe fell under Bonaparte's rule as he won victory after victory. Through humiliating treaties and shrewd alliances, Napoleon strengthened his European dominance. Eventually, his relatives and military men ruled over foreign governments throughout the continent.

| Arc de Triomphe (Napoleon being crowned)

The French emperor actually changed the map of Europe. Forcing the emperor of the Holy Roman Empire to give up his throne and become emperor of Austria, Napoleon abolished the Holy Roman Empire. The states of Germany and Italy were consolidated and the French military spread throughout the land.

His great success was his undoing—he instilled the spirit of nationalism in the minds and hearts of Europeans. At first the French were warmly received by oppressed people seeking freedom from harsh, absolute governments. However, the warmth did not last. The French conquerors became arrogant and overbearing. The French policy of taxation to support its occupation forces was extremely unpopular. Also, troops were quartered in individual homes, and foreign men were drafted to service in the French army. As French troops lingered on foreign soil, an attitude of resentment grew among the people of other nations. They developed a strong desire to be ruled by their own government and be led by people of their own nation. Napoleon had fostered the nationalism that would drive him from power.

The French blockade of Europe led to further dissent by people on the continent. Though unable to keep all English trading ships away, enough business was being lost to infuriate European merchants. Those who cooperated with England were severely punished. Napoleon was so obsessed with enforcing the blockade that he dismissed his brother Louis, king of Holland, for his failure to enforce it. Even the pope was placed under arrest for expressing his disapproval of the blockade. Punishment was continually handed out to European countries who rebelled against the blockade and French rule.

As ruler of Europe, Napoleon's position seemed secure. However, Napoleon's army, was now filled with drafted foreigners and was a growing threat to his position. Not only were his soldiers unwilling to follow their French leader, they also longed to overthrow him.

In 1808, Spain revolted against Napoleon's brother Joseph, king of Spain. With the help of British and Portuguese troops, the Spanish drove out the French, capturing Madrid in 1812. The Spanish then drew up their own constitution, throwing off the shackles of French domination and persecution.

Napoleon's downfall came when he decided to invade Russia. Czar Alexander I disregarded the French blockade and encouraged trade with England. Growing increasingly less tolerant of those who were not in agreement with his blockade, Napoleon declared war on the Russians in 1812. Raising an army of over six hundred thousand men, he pushed the Russians all the way back to Moscow. Although the drive was successful, it was costly; many of his men were either killed by guerrilla forces or left behind in towns to guard supplies. The Russians had wisely retreated, burning and destroying everything as they went. They left nothing standing that Napoleon might be able to use. The Russians knew that the French army, which included Germans, Italians, Dutch, and other Europeans, would become spread out and difficult to supply.

Having captured Moscow in September, Napoleon was faced with a difficult choice. He could either continue chasing the shrewdly retreating Russians, stay in Moscow for the winter, or return to Western Europe. Because winter quarters for the troops in Moscow were insufficient and supply lines were particularly vulnerable, Napoleon chose to return to Western Europe. Not long afterward, Bonaparte realized the disastrous consequences of his decision.

| Napoleon

A combination of the severe Russian winter and the guerrilla harassment of the pursuing Russian soldiers took a heavy toll on Napoleon's forces. Over two-thirds of his men were lost by the time the army reached Germany in December.

Upon his return to France, Napoleon found that the nations of Europe had united to face him in his moment of weakness. Napoleon gathered yet another army to meet the combined troops of Austrians, Russians, British, and Swedish in battle. At this Battle of Nations fought at Leipzig, Germany, in October, 1813, Napoleon was finally defeated. When Paris was captured in March, 1814, Napoleon was forced to surrender his throne.

The would-be emperor of Europe was granted a pension and went to live on the island of Elba off the western coast of Italy. He agreed to live there as sovereign for the rest of his life. France's boundaries were returned to what they were in 1792, before Napoleon's expansion. The monarchy was restored under Louis XVIII, the brother of the king executed by the National Convention. He had to recognize the changes brought about by the revolution, however. A constitution was established that set up a limited monarchy and absolutism was not restored.

One year after his defeat, Napoleon returned to France on March 1, 1815, with a small band of loyal followers to regain his lost power. Still popular with many, he received support from the French people on his return. Troops sent by Louis XVIII quickly turned their allegiance to their former emperor. The king fled the country, and Bonaparte entered Paris in triumph without firing a shot. He announced his intention of restoring a constitutional government in France.

Although France did not strongly oppose Napoleon's return, that was not the case with her fellow European nations. Armies from Prussia, Great Britain, and Holland immediately joined to meet Napoleon's forces at Waterloo, Belgium, in June of 1815. The three day battle brought Bonaparte's final defeat and ended his short return to power, known as the Hundred Days War. Napoleon was banished, under guard, to the South Atlantic island of St. Helena, 5,000 miles from Europe, where he died in 1821 at the age of fifty-two.

The French Revolution had not only made a lasting mark on France, but also on Europe and the world. Frenchmen enjoyed greater liberty and equality in 1815 than in the years before 1789. Even Napoleon could not dampen the free thinking that he spread from France throughout Europe. However, the changes in France were not as stable as in England and America. France would continue to have revolts and changes in government for many, many years.

✎ **Complete the following sentences.**

3.27 A militarily forced takeover, such as Napoleon's, is called a(n) _____ .

3.28 Napoleon took over the government of France on _____ .

3.29 The years of Napoleon are referred to as the _____ of Europe.

3.30 A strong feeling of loyalty toward one's country is called _____ .

3.31 The organization of French laws under Bonaparte was called _____

_____ .

3.32 Napoleon's return to France in 1815 is known as _____ .

3.33 In 1804 Napoleon declared France a(n) a. _____ and himself

b. _____ .

Underline the answer that *does not* fit.

3.34 French reforms under Napoleon's rule included

    a. economic and social reforms,   b. Oath of the Tennis Court,

    c. the Code Napoleon,   d. Bank of France, and

    e. an educational system.

3.35 In his quest for control of Europe, Napoleon

    a. blockaded England,   b. conquered mainland Europe,

    c. defeated Syria,   d. abolished the Holy Roman Empire, and

    e. consolidated the states in Germany and Italy.

3.36 Factors causing Napoleon's European conquests to resent him included

    a. taxing to support soldiers,   b. quartering troops in homes,

    c. drafting foreigners,   d. French blockade of Europe, and

    e. Code Napoleon.

3.37 Factors leading to Napoleon's defeat included

    a. Portuguese revolt,   b. rising nationalism,

    c. Spanish revolt,   d. invasion of Russia, and

    e. decision to return from Russia.

Give the significance of the following battles.

3.38 Battle off Cape Trafalgar _____

_____

_____

3.39 Invasion of Russia _____

_____

_____

3.40 Battle of the Nations _____

_____

_____

3.41 Battle of Waterloo _____

_____

_____

Answer this question.

3.42 What changes had the French Revolution brought to the life of the common man in France?

_____

_____

_____

_____

_____

_____

Complete the following activity.

3.43 Draw maps that show Europe before, during, and after the Napoleonic Era (use an encyclopedia or online resource for help).

TEACHER CHECK _____ _____
initials   date

🔄 **Before taking this last Self Test, you may want to do one or more of these self checks.**

1. _____ Read the objectives. Determine if you can do them.
2. _____ Restudy the material related to any objectives that you cannot do.
3. _____ Use the **SQ3R** study procedure to review the material.
        a. **S**can the sections.
        b. **Q**uestion yourself again (review the questions you wrote initially).
        c. **R**ead to answer your questions.
        d. **R**ecite the answers to yourself.
        e. **R**eview areas you didn't understand.
4. _____ Review all vocabulary, activities, and Self Tests, writing a correct answer for each wrong answer.

SELF TEST 3

Match these items (each answer, 2 points).

3.01	_____ Cromwell	a. first prime minister of England
3.02	_____ Cornwallis	b. British commander at Lexington
3.03	_____ Washington	c. leader of the Jacobin Club
3 04	_____ Cavaliers	d. commander of Continental army
3.05	_____ Roundheads	e. famous French writer
3.06	_____ Walpole	f. British commander at Yorktown
3.07	_____ Napoleon	g. supporters of Charles I
3.08	_____ Danton	h. English antimonarchists
3.09	_____ Voltaire	i. Italian emperor of France
3.010	_____ Gage	j. famous French theologian
		k. Roundhead leader in English Revolution

Complete the following sentences (each answer, 3 points).

3.011 England's political parties under Charles II were the a. _____
and the b. _____ .

3.012 The English Revolution put a. _____ in control of English affairs,
with the b. _____ more of a figurehead.

3.013 English a. _____ and b. _____
infuriated the colonists against England.

3.014 American victory in 1781 came when a. _____ surrendered at
b. _____ .

3.015 The estates of France were the clergy, a. _____ , and the
b. _____ .

3.016 The _____ declared much
needed personal freedoms for the French.

3.017 The military _____ greatly strengthened the French army under
the National Convention.

3.018 At first, Napoleon ruled as a. _____ in France; in 1804 he became

b. _____ .

3.019 The organization of French laws under Napoleon was called the _____ .

3.020 Napoleon's short return to power in 1815 is known as the _____ .

Answer true or false (each answer, 1 point).

3.021 _____ Separatists and Puritans were groups of Presbyterians.

3.022 _____ The Habeas Corpus Act and the Act of Separation brought personal freedoms to the English.

3.023 _____ The branches of American government are the legislative and judicial branches.

3.024 _____ Amendments and balance of power are strong points of America's Constitution.

3.025 _____ French writers and the American Revolution inspired the French to move toward their own revolution.

3.026 _____ The Oath of the Tennis Court was taken by Napoleon's soldiers.

3.027 _____ The Consulate brought weak, unorganized leadership to France.

3.028 _____ French taxation and the blockade of Europe caused resentment among her conquered nations.

3.029 _____ Napoleon made great reforms in French banking, education, and law.

3.030 _____ The invasion of Austria brought the start of defeat to Napoleon.

Write the letter for the correct answer on each line (each answer, 2 points).

3.031 Factors during the reign of Louis XV which hastened the coming Revolution were _____ .
a. laziness of the king, desperate financial situation, and Declaration of the Rights of Man
b. desperate financial situation, Declaration of the Rights of Man, and inspiration of American Revolution
c. laziness of the king, desperate financial situation, and inspiration of American Revolution
d. laziness of the king, Declaration of the Rights of Man, and inspiration of American Revolution

3.032 French legislative bodies included the _____ .
a. National Assembly, National Convention, and Estates-General
b. National Convention, Estates-General, and Directory
c. National Assembly, National Convention, and Directory
d. National Assembly, Estates-General, and Directory

3.033 Steps leading to Napoleon's takeover of France included _____ .

    a. military victories making him a national hero, excellent military skill, fear and chaos of French life, and defeat of Syria

    b. excellent military skill, fear and chaos of French life, defeat of Syria, and weakness of the Directory's leadership

    c. military victories making him a national hero, excellent military skill, defeat of Syria, and weakness of the Directory's leadership

    d. military victories making him a national hero, excellent military skill, fear and chaos of French life, and weakness of the Directory's leadership

3.034 In his quest for control of Europe, Napoleon _____ .

    a. conquered mainland Europe, blockaded Europe from England, abolished the Holy Roman Empire, and consolidated the states in Germany and Italy

    b. blockaded Europe from England, abolished the Holy Roman Empire, consolidated the states in Germany and Italy, and smothered nationalism

    c. conquered mainland Europe, blockaded Europe from England, consolidated the states in Germany and Italy, and smothered nationalism

    d. conquered mainland Europe, abolished the Holy Roman Empire, consolidated the states in Germany and Italy, and smothered nationalism

3.035 The revolutions in England, America, and France _____ .

    a. abolished the monarchy in each, gave the people new freedoms, and gave people more voice in their government

    b. gave the people new freedoms, gave people more voice in their government, and brought greater equality among the people

    c. abolished the monarchy in each, gave the people new freedoms, and brought greater equality among the people

    d. abolished the monarchy in each, gave people more voice in their government, and brought greater equality among the people

Complete the following activities (each problem, 3 points).

3.036 What factors and events led to the defeat of Napoleon?

_____

_____

_____

_____

3.037 Give at least four factors and events that led to the increasing unrest and coming revolution during Louis XVI's rule.

_____

_____

_____

_____

3.038 What factors and traits of Napoleon made the French people turn to him for leadership and hopeful end to the insecurity of their daily life?

_____

_____

_____

3.039 Give the significance of the following battles.

a. Cromwell's victory over the Cavaliers _____

_____

_____

b. Battle of Lexington _____

_____

_____

c. Battle of Yorktown _____

_____

_____

d. Battle of Nations _____

_____

_____

e. Battle of Waterloo _____

_____

_____

80 / 100   **SCORE** _____   **TEACHER** _____ _____
                                                  initials   date

Before taking the LIFEPAC Test, you may want to do one or more of these self checks.

1. _____ Read the objectives. Check to see if you can do them.

2. _____ Restudy the material related to any objectives that you cannot do.

3. _____ Use the **SQ3R** study procedure to review the material.

4. _____ Review activities, Self Tests, and LIFEPAC vocabulary words.

5. _____ Restudy areas of weakness indicated by the last Self Test.

GLOSSARY

absolutism .... A system or form of government in which the ruler has unrestricted power.

Anglican .... The Church of England, or a member of the Church of England.

aristocracy .... The upper or privileged class.

Calvinist .... A follower of the French theologian, John Calvin.

Cavalier .... A supporter of Charles I.

coalition .... An alliance of nations for a common purpose.

commonwealth .... A government in which the sovereignty is given to the people.

conscription .... A draft, compulsory enrollment of men for military service.

coup d'état .... A sudden seizure of government.

divine right .... A king's belief that his rule is God's will.

émigrés .... An emigrant, one who fled to escape the French Revolution.

estates .... The social classes of France.

executive .... The head of state managing the administrative affairs of a nation.

guillotine .... A death instrument in France, consisting of a weighted blade that slides down between two vertical guides and beheads the victim.

judicial .... The branch of government which enforces the laws, making judgments in courts of justice.

legislative .... The lawmaking branch of government.

Lettres de cachet .... Sealed letters, French royal orders for the imprisonment of some person.

mercantilism .... The establishment of colonies by a country, requiring the colony to support the mother country with raw materials and manufactured goods.

militia .... Citizens enrolled in the military, called out for emergencies.

monarchy .... Government by a hereditary sovereign with complete control.

nationalism	Devotion to one's own country and its interests.
Parliament	The supreme legislature of Great Britain.
presbyter	An elder in the Presbyterian Church.
proprietor	A person given the exclusive right to full administrative power over a territory under royal grant.
Roundheads	Members of the anti-monarch, pro-Parliament party in England.
Stuart	A royal family of England beginning with James I.
Tory	A member of the English political party succeeding the Cavaliers who wanted a strong king.
Tudor	The royal family of England, including Elizabeth I.
Whig	A member of the English political party succeeding the Roundheads who wanted the real power in the hands of Parliament.